R o

Bar & Nightlife Guide

LOS ANGELES

ROMMELMANN'S

Bar & Nightlife Guide

Nancy Rommelmann

 An LA Weekly Book for St. Martin's Press 🕮 New York

ROMMELMANN'S LOS ANGELES BAR AND NIGHTLIFE GUIDE. Copyright © 2001 by Nancy Rommelmann. All rights reserved. Printed in the United States of America. No part of this book may be used or reproduced in any manner whatsoever without written permission except in the case of brief quotations embodied in critical articles or reviews. For information, address St. Martin's Press, 175 Fifth Avenue, New York, N.Y. 10010.

LA Weekly Books is a trademark of LA Weekly Media, Inc.

www.stmartins.com

Design by Fritz Metsch

Library of Congress Cataloging-in-Publication Data

Rommelmann, Nancy.
  [Los Angeles bar & nightlife guide]
  Rommelmann's Los Angeles bar & nightlife guide / Nancy Rommelmann.
    p. cm.
  ISBN 0-312-26936-6
  1. Bars (Drinking establishments)—California—Los Angeles—Guidebooks. I. Title: Los Angeles bar and nightlife guide. II. Title.

TX950.57.C2 R66 2001
647.95794'94—dc21   2001019176

First Edition: May 2001

1 3 5 7 9 10 8 6 4 2

Contents

Acknowledgments
vii

Introduction
ix

Cautionary Note
xi

BARS AND CLUBS
1

LATE-NIGHT EATING
103

BARS, CLUBS, AND DINING BY LOCATION
121

BARS AND CLUBS, BY TYPE OF MUSIC
129

BARS AND CLUBS BY TYPE OF SCENE AND OTHER CATEGORIES
135

Notes
145

Acknowledgments

Thanks to my agent, Laura Dail; to my editor at LA Weekly Books/St. Martin's Press, Elizabeth Beier, and to the magazine editors who've given me nightlife gigs: at *Buzz*, Allan Mayer and Renee Vogel, and at *Los Angeles*, Michael Caruso and Mark Horowitz, and for editorial assistance, Diana Yassanye. Thanks to all the bar owners who've stood me drinks. And special thanks to my longtime drinking buddies: Chris, Hillary, Sarah, Dario, my sweetheart Din, and my dad, Richard Rommelmann, former New York bartender and all-around good guy, to whom this book is dedicated.

Introduction

When I started covering nightlife, in 1995, the question I most often heard was, "You get paid to go out and drink?!" Well, yes. My job as a columnist for *Buzz* and, later, *Los Angeles* was to check out what was going on after 9 P.M., and to write about it. I received a lot of grateful phone calls about the places I covered, but when I'd ask how the caller liked, say, Babe's & Ricky's Inn, the person would invariably stutter, "Oh, I haven't gone yet..." Which is when I realized that, while people do not necessarily want to go, they do want to know, as there are few situations more frustrating than having the time/cash/inclination to step out and not a clue as to where. After fielding 30,000 requests for additional advice, my public service contribution was two pages outlining 20 places I liked, which I gave to friends, who began copying them to give to their friends, all of whom called me after the pages, crammed beneath the car seat, became too tattered to read. Which gave me an idea...

With close to 200 listings, plus 40 late-night spots to eat, this guide is handier than a handout, and certainly more comprehensive, with a lot of cross-referencing, so that when you get to that blues club you liked so much years ago and realize it's now a mini-mall, you'll be able to find a place to your liking within the same area code/scope of experience.

Just want to take a look? Many of the listings include a Web address, so you can check out a spot before checking it out. Like staying until last call? The headings will tell you whether the venue stays open as late as the law allows (2 A.M.). Want a bite with that shot? The guide lets you know if, and what, you'll be eating. How about a cigarette? Well, that's tougher: since California banned smoking indoors in bars, smokers have been scrambling to find places with patios; the good news (for smokers) is that many establishments are adding outdoor spaces. There is also a whole bunch of bars that don't enforce the law; you'll know which ones they are by the MY CUSTOMERS ARE MY BUSINESS signs and billows of attendant smoke. I, for one, think the law is a terrible idea; however, if you're asked to put out a cigarette, do management a favor and stub it, as the fines imposed can literally put a place out of business.

I have not covered every bar and club in Los Angeles, but only the ones I find interesting, memorable, or fun (or, in a few instances, so dreadful one should be warned against them). Undoubtedly, I have overlooked your favorite, which I'm happy to hear about. Until then.

Cautionary Note

The nightlife scene in Los Angeles is constantly in flux: last month's biggest deal is closed by the LAFD; the reliably quiet old man bar turns into a hunting-lodge hipster joint; the surf band that's been playing every Sunday for five years at the same Tiki lounge isn't playing there anymore. All by way of saying: if you're counting on a specific scene, do yourself a favor and call ahead, or check the club listings section of the *LA Weekly*.

As to cost, I've employed the old $:

$—$12 or less
$$—$12 to $25
$$$—$25 and above

The $s do not include food, my prognostication as to how many singles you'll tuck in the dancer's G-string, or exceptional cover charges, but indicate the average amount you'll spend for two drinks and a healthy tip.

Bars and Clubs

AKBAR

4356 SUNSET BLVD. (AT FOUNTAIN), SILVERLAKE (323) 665-6810. OPEN NIGHTLY, 6 P.M.–2 A.M. FULL BAR. 21 AND OVER. NO COVER. NO FOOD. $$.

It's not clear whether this mosquelike bar faces Mecca, but Akbar (purportedly named after one of Matt Groening's be-fezzed *Life in Hell* characters) does draw a devoted crowd of gay and/or arty Silverlakers happy to hang out close to home. The ocean-blue interior, Casbah-like rear room, and his and her nude oil portraits give Akbar a mildly erotic/exotic vibe. A good neighborhood spot in which to grab an early drink, but be warned: it can get VERY LOUD later in the evening.

ALL STAR LANES

4459 EAGLE ROCK BLVD. (AT YORK), EAGLE ROCK (323) 254-2579. OPEN SUN.–THURS., NOON–11 P.M.; FRI., NOON–MIDNIGHT; SAT., NOON–1:30 A.M. FULL BAR. ALL AGES, EXCEPT IN THE LOUNGE, 21 AND OVER. COVER ON SAT. FOOD (SNACK BAR). $.

Yer local, colorful, SoCal bowling alley, except on Saturday nights, when it's transformed for "Bowl-a-Rama/Rockabilly Night." The $12 cover gets you two hours of bowling, four (or so) live rockabilly bands, and eye-candy: lots of Murray's pomade, bangs curled à la Betty Page, fifties duds, and intricate tat-work. Unless they're rock-a-babes in training, leave the kids at home, as the place gets loud. Lively alternative to the packed-on-Saturday-night bar scene.

AL'S BAR

305 S. HEWITT (AT TRACTION), DOWNTOWN LA (213) 625-9703. WWW.ALSBAR.NET. OPEN TUES.–SUN., 6 P.M.–2 A.M.;

CLOSED MON. BEER AND WINE ONLY. 21 AND OVER. COVER $5 (FREE TUES. AND WED.). NO FOOD. $.

When everything else in Los Angeles seems to have been packaged and produced to a digestible pulp, you can count on Al's to give it to you straight. Live punk and/or garage every night—some great, some hilariously inept—in two graffiti-covered rooms that proudly wear 20 years of wanton destruction. The crowd appreciates and incites mayhem; I don't think I've ever been to Al's when someone wasn't spitting, shooting off Silly String, and/or taking off his or her clothes. The music's loud and screechy, and the crowd always seems buzzed-up and happy—and grateful that Al's keeps it good and grungy. Not for everyone, amen.

THE ATLAS SUPPER CLUB

3760 WILSHIRE BLVD. (AT WESTERN), LA (213) 380-8400. WWW.CLUBATLAS.COM. OPEN TUES.–SAT., 6 P.M.–2 A.M.; CLOSED SUN. AND MON. NIGHTS. FULL BAR. 21 AND OVER. COVER VARIES. FOOD ("GLOBAL CUISINE"). $$.

The Atlas is so vast, and the ceilings are so high, that I think of it as the Grand Central of clubs. A massive glass partition etched with a map of the world separates the long bar from the supper club and stage—the sort of swank and sparkling room where you might expect to see Fred and Ginger come tap-tap-tapping from behind the wings. What you'll see instead: spoken word, speakeasy, Latin lounge, hip-hop. A wonderful place, with one caveat: early in the evening, the crowd from the nearby office towers sometimes seems a little eager to embark on a singles scene. If this isn't your thing, skip the after-work mingling and make reservations for dinner and a show.

BABE'S & RICKY'S INN

4339 LEIMERT BLVD. (TWO BLOCKS EAST OF CRENSHAW), LEIMERT PARK (323) 295-9112. OPEN WED.–MON., 8 P.M.–2 A.M.; SUN., 6:30 P.M.–2 A.M.; CLOSED TUES. BEER AND WINE ONLY. 21 AND OVER. COVER VARIES. FOOD (FRIED CHICKEN, BARBECUE). $$.

When the original Babe's & Ricky's, formerly located on Central Avenue, closed several years ago, blues aficionados felt all but abandoned. Where else could they hear music of near-religious intensity in a room devoid of signed guitars and $40 covers and white folks slapping the table out of time? Then, salvation: regal septuagenarian owner Laura Gross, of the jewel-tone muumuus and reputation for god-mothering legions of blues players, had simply relocated to Leimert Park. The 'hood's a lot nicer, the room's bigger and cozier, and the live music still is and always will be the real thing. Great place to hunker down with some cold beer and some hot and painful blues. Don't even think about not ordering some Phillip's Barbecue, which Babe's & Ricky's carries in from next door.

THE BAKED POTATO

3787 CAHUENGA BLVD. WEST (AT LANKERSHIM), NORTH HOLLYWOOD (818) 980-1615. WWW.THEBAKEDPOTATO.COM. OPEN NIGHTLY, 7 P.M.–2 A.M. FULL BAR. ALL AGES. COVER VARIES. FOOD (POTATOES AND FIXINGS). $$.

If you're of the mind that good jazz doesn't need a lot of window dressing, you'll enjoy this low-key club, where the only distractions from the music are the optional and enormous baked potatoes, which, with any of 21 accompaniments, take an hour to eat, just about as long as a set by the jazz, blues, and fusion groups that play at 9:30 P.M.

and 11:30 P.M. Acts tend to be mellow, with an emphasis on vocalists, acoustic guitar, and piano. Pressure-free, smooth clientele, and if the dark woody decor circa 1972 (when pianist Don Randi opened the place) feels a little confined, check out the Hollywood branch, which has something the original doesn't: windows.

THE BAKED POTATO HOLLYWOOD

6266 SUNSET BLVD. (AT VINE), HOLLYWOOD (323) 461-6400. WWW.THEBAKEDPOTATO.COM. OPEN NIGHTLY, 7 P.M.–2 A.M. FULL BAR. ALL AGES. COVER VARIES. FOOD (POTATOES AND FIXINGS). $$.

Same as above, except larger and brighter.

BARFLY

8730 SUNSET BLVD. (TWO BLOCKS WEST OF LA CIENEGA) WEST HOLLYWOOD (310) 360-9490. OPEN MON.–SAT., 7:30 P.M.–2 A.M.; CLOSED SUN. FULL BAR. 21 AND OVER. NO COVER. FOOD (ECLECTIC AND SUSHI). $$$.

The very idea of writing about Barfly makes me weary, but here goes: despite having a ten-foot photo of writer Charles Bukowski in the entryway, they'd never let the legendary boozer into this large, expensive-looking bar/restaurant, which, with its busy bar scene, high-end dining, sushi bar, and techno-groove beat tries to be all things to all people. That is, if they're very beautiful and very rich, or know how to give the impression they are. The treatment begins at the door, where the guy manning the velvet rope feigns a debilitating eye injury that prevents him from seeing customers displaying too little of whatever élan it is Barfly is looking for. Those who make the cut get in and get to hang out with each other. Let them.

BAR MARMONT

8171 SUNSET BLVD. (ONE BLOCK WEST OF CRESCENT HEIGHTS), WEST HOLLYWOOD (323) 650-0575. OPEN MON.–SAT., 6 P.M.–2 A.M.; SUN., 7 P.M.–2 A.M. FULL BAR. ALL AGES. NO COVER. FOOD (ECLECTIC). $$.

Liking or disliking Bar Marmont depends on one's worldview: if you are of the considered opinion that a contemptuous door-guy allowing you in raises your standing in society/your self-esteem; that paying $7 for a beer is an okay thing; that butterflies on the ceiling, porcelain cats on the bar, and odd swimming pool acoustics are a style statement; that watching patrons alternately worry about what their hair looks like and chatter on cell phones is a good time, then, by all means, go to Bar Marmont, a bar and restaurant that has the dubious honor of remaining trendy despite, or perhaps because of, the above. If, on the other hand, you avoid such places like the plague, visiting them but once a year for research purposes or because a perverse, voyeuristic friend insists, you will do yourself a favor to skip Bar Marmont.

BARNEY'S BEANERY

8447 SANTA MONICA BLVD. (TWO BLOCKS EAST OF LA CIENEGA), WEST HOLLYWOOD (323) 654-2287. OPEN DAILY, 11 A.M.–2 A.M. ALL AGES. FULL BAR. NO COVER. FOOD (AMERICAN). $$.

In 1986, when I first came to LA, I hung out at Barney's because I didn't know where else to go. I liked the bar, a narrow drinking man's room that smelled like beer-soaked wood where I saw actor Michael Sarandon occupying the same stool each time I stopped in. The food was pretty awful (chili on everything; canned mushrooms in the spinach salad), but there were a lot of pool tables, and, if you didn't mind playing with guys who wore bandanas à la Axl Rose, you could painlessly if aimlessly while away six months' worth of afternoons. Except for the removal of a gay-baiting sign several years ago (the place is, after all, in the center of WeHo), Barney's hasn't changed in 15 years. Probably it never will change. A chummy spot in which to grab a drink/watch the game if you live in the neighborhood; otherwise, seek higher ground.

BAR VERMONT

1712 N. VERMONT AVE. (½ BLOCK NORTH OF HOLLYWOOD), LOS FELIZ (323) 661-6163. OPEN SUN.–THURS., 5:30 P.M.–11:30 P.M.; FRI. & SAT., 5:30 P.M.–1:30 A.M. FULL BAR. 21 AND OVER. NO COVER. FOOD (ECLECTIC/AMERICAN). $$.

What Michael G. and Manuel Mesta have brought to their wonderfully warm and always delicious restaurant Vermont, they now bring next door, to Bar Vermont. A stunning room with vaulted ceilings, a twenty-foot-long marble bar, and massive candles creating a lot of shadow play throughout, the feel (if this isn't oxymoronic) is both monastic and comfortable. With lots of couches and lounges on which to loll, and enjoy the delectable bar offerings (oysters, *bruschetta*, seared duck dumplings, and oh! that caramel custard), locals have made it the bar to be at in Los Feliz, and yet Bar Vermont is also a superb destination: You can bring anyone to this sanctuary of peace and plenty, and enjoy the kudos of having introduced them to one of the nicest places in town.

B.B. KING'S BLUES CLUB

1000 UNIVERSAL CENTER DR., UNIVERSAL CITY (818) 622-5464. OPEN DAILY, 4 P.M.–2 A.M. 21 AND OVER. FULL BAR. COVER, $10–$12. FOOD (SOUTHERN). $$.

The way I heard it, when Robert Johnson sold his soul to the devil in exchange for the brimstone needed to play the blues, he was standing on a dark crossroads in the Mississippi Delta. How this fervent exchange evolved into the money-sucking corporate blues clubs LA sports is beyond me. Unlike the truly hellish House of Blues, however, B.B. King's maintains its sanctity by booking excellent national acts, by hosting a spirited and popular Sunday gospel brunch, and by boasting the occasional appearance of B.B. King himself. The main problem with the place is that it is located in the fetid candy-land that is CityWalk, which means you must crawl through traffic, shell out heavily to park, and traverse a gauntlet of tourist traps and an 18-theater multiplex before you even get to the club. Go with out-of-towners who think this sort of thing is part of the fun.

BEAUTY BAR

1638 CAHUENGA AVE. (HALF A BLOCK SOUTH OF HOLLYWOOD), HOLLYWOOD (323) 464-7676. OPEN SAT.-WED., 8 P.M.-2 A.M.; THURS. AND FRI., 6 P.M.-2 A.M. 21 AND OVER. FULL BAR. NO COVER. NO FOOD. $$.

When the first Beauty Bar opened in New York in the early nineties, it was in a former beauty salon in the East Village. The room had hairdryers and barber chairs and jars of blue Barbicide, and the crowd was local and punky: lots of bleached hair and ratty fishnets. The owners followed the formula in San Francisco a few years later. Then LA got its own Beauty Bar, which is more luxurious and stylistically precise and a wee bit more uptight than its predecessors. No torn stockings here: the girlies favor cocktail dresses, and the guys all look as though they shop at the same slightly fey suit shop. However, the room (once an Indian restaurant) is a treasure: styling chairs and hood-dryers (in which you'll always see at least one guy resting his head; women, who've experienced the real thing, don't bother), along with a mirrored mini-salon, where early in the evening you can get a manicure and a martini for $10. The beautiful lighting is worth noting: Moderne fixtures flatteringly located throughout the room, and mounted within suspended dryer bonnets, which, from a distance, look like enormous, exotic butterflies. Very much the place to be and be seen (particularly for Westsiders, who find Hollywood's other 100 bars slightly . . . seamy).

THE BIGFOOT LODGE

3172 LOS FELIZ BLVD. (AT GLENFELIZ), ATWATER VILLAGE (323) 662-9227. WWW.BIGFOOTLODGE.COM. OPEN NIGHTLY, 8 P.M.–2 A.M. FULL BAR. 21 AND OVER. NO COVER. NO FOOD. $$.

Probably the only bar in LA where you'd look at home wearing L.L. Bean duck boots, this sizable lounge-cum-Canadian-lodge is bisected by a National Forest road sign reading "Saskatchewan," and is even tricked up with a diorama of Bambi in the entryway. The campfire theme carries over to the cocktails: Girl Scout Cookie (crème de menthe and Irish cream), Toasted Marshmallow, Dudley Do-Right (Canadian Club and Amaretto). Whether it's the novel aesthetic or Angelenos' subliminal longing for (a facsimile of) cold weather, the Bigfoot draws a wildly eclectic group: last time I was there, a plumbing contractor celebrating his birthday bought the house a round, a full-out rockabilly couple sang along with Patsy Cline, and a half-dozen goth kids sat, expressionless and silent, on several comfy couches in the rear lounge area. Excellent Eastside lounge (and so cute!), but absolutely smash-packed on weekends.

BLACKLITE COCKTAIL ROOM

1159 N. Western Ave. (one block north of Santa Monica), Hollywood (323) 469-0211. Open daily, 6 a.m.–2 a.m. Full bar. 21 and over. No cover. No food. $.

I no doubt flatter myself by claiming that I find very few bars scary, but this is one of them. Rough trade and street people frequent this boxy, serious-drinking bar, whose tinsel-covered ceiling is pretty much trumped by a long, oddly placed center table that looks like something on which to eviscerate hogs. But don't let that stop you.

THE BLUE ROOM

916 S. San Fernando Blvd. (at Alameda), Burbank (323) 849-2779. Open daily, 10 a.m.–2 a.m. Full bar. 21 and over. No cover. No food. $.

This quirky oasis off the 5 freeway is a real wild card. Comfy-captain's-quarters motif, friendly bartenders, San Fernando Road regulars, a giant elephant brandishing a gun on the roof (oh, don't ask why). Good place to get out of the city and huddle with a sweetheart (the white leather booths are high backed, huge, and squishy), play darts with the locals, or watch a Sunday afternoon ball game.

THE BLUE SALOON

4657 Lankershim Blvd. (at Kling), North Hollywood (818) 766-4644. Open daily, noon–2 a.m. Full bar. 21 and over. Cover $5. No food. $.

Though they have all kinds of live music here—soul, rock, reggae—I always think of the Blue Saloon as a country place where the patrons are kicked-back and casual, given to playing pool and talking back to the big screen when the Lakers fall behind. Typical bar decor (i.e., neon signs and video games), nice folks behind the bar, congenial working-Joe customers. A destination if you're partial to who's onstage; otherwise, a solid local joint.

BOARDNER'S

1652 CHEROKEE AVE. (AT HOLLYWOOD), HOLLYWOOD (323) 462-9621. OPEN DAILY, 11 A.M.–2 A.M. FULL BAR. 21 AND OVER. AFTER 10 P.M., COVER VARIES. FOOD (AMERICAN). $.

Boardner's opened in the 1940s, and looks it: the floor and carpet are worn, the booths appear to have accommodated a billion behinds, the restaurant serves the sort of Continental cuisine one finds from Portland to Portland. Not surprisingly, Boardner's is home to a great group of regulars—old-timers with a lively interest in and loquacity on topics of the day. Further props to Boardner's: several nights a week, different promoters take over the dining room and adjacent patio after 10 P.M., running funk, soul, and goth clubs and a heavy dance scene. Interesting, hardcore clubbers make up the bulk of late-night patronage, ensuring good local color anytime you stop in.

BOB BURNS

202 WILSHIRE BLVD. (AT 2ND ST.), SANTA MONICA (310) 393-6777. OPEN MON.–THURS., 11:30 A.M.–11:30 P.M.; FRI. AND SAT., 11:30 A.M.–1:00 A.M.; SUN., 11:00 A.M.–11:00 P.M. FULL BAR. ALL AGES. NO COVER. FOOD (STEAKS). $$.

Mellow American restaurant and lounge featuring live music Sunday through Tuesday evenings, by Howlett "Smitty" Smith, a blind pianist who's been playing at Bob Burns for 25 years. (Wednesday to Friday, chanteuse Amelia Haygood performs.) Smith is a real smoothie, with an easy charm one associates with cocktail culture of yore, and his repertoire and repartee draw listeners to the piano, à la a sentimental scene in a forties film—casually elegant ladies and gents sipping scotch and asking Smitty to play their song, which he will do. The crowd tends to be older, the sort of folks who grew up understanding that a good steak every night is both a liberty and a joy.

BOB'S FROLIC ROOM. *See listing under "Frolic Room."*

BRASS MONKEY
659 S. MARIPOSA AVE. (HALF A BLOCK SOUTH OF WILSHIRE), MID-WILSHIRE (213) 381-7047. OPEN DAILY, 11 A.M.–2 A.M. FULL BAR. 21 AND OVER. NO COVER. FOOD (AMERICAN). $$.

No matter what I write about the Brass Monkey, it will not equal the experience of being there. But let me try: assorted codgers, middle managers, and fanatical karaokers mingling in what looks like a ski hostel/early seventies pickup bar. The oddball aesthetics have a way of warping space and time. Example: after letting a man who looked and spoke like William Burroughs buy me several hundred bourbons, I swore I was a first-wave career gal (Mary Richards sans morals) trying to navigate the singles scene. When I heard the Fifth Dimension playing, I believed I'd fallen into some sort of cosmic wormhole, until I saw a small white girl in an Ann Taylor suit belting out "Last Night I Didn't Get to Sleep..." as though her next promotion depended on it. Serious and raucous karaoke scene, with tuxedoed MC and the best selection of songs I've ever heard. An absorbing experience for those who think LA has lost its ability to surprise them.

BURGUNDY ROOM

1621½ CAHUENGA BLVD. (A HALF BLOCK SOUTH OF HOLLYWOOD), HOLLYWOOD (323) 465-7530. OPEN NIGHTLY, 8 P.M.–2 A.M. FULL BAR. 21 AND OVER. NO COVER. NO FOOD. $$.

Once a deep-dark, beer-and-wine-only affair, Burgundy Room has blossomed into what may be the best-looking bar in Hollywood: beautiful, traditional shotgun layout, flattering amber lighting, very nice bartenders, good liquor at a fair price, coolness without trying too hard, and patrons who don't take themselves so very seriously. A perfect place to hunker down with a couple of friends and a few dozen cocktails and spend the evening discussing how good life can be. One of my favorites.

CANTER'S KIBITZ ROOM

419 N. FAIRFAX AVE. (ONE BLOCK NORTH OF BEVERLY BLVD.), LA (323) 651-2030. OPEN DAILY, NOON–2 A.M. FULL BAR. 21 AND OVER. NO COVER. FOOD (DELICATESSEN). $.

I believe people have big feelings about Canter's because it's the only delicatessen between Fairfax and MacArthur Park. I cannot, however, tell you exactly why Canter's Kibitz Room, the bar attached to the deli by a big window (through which you can, fishbowl-style, watch irritable, blue-haired waitresses deliver blintzes and borscht) remains popular. Something to do with rock 'n' roll, judging by the patrons, whose leathery beach-boy complexions and mullet hairdos give them away as having had a close brush with fame sometime between 1966 and 1982. It's sort of heartbreaking, which perhaps goes some way to explaining the fondness people feel for this quasi-seedy room. Live music, mostly rock, on the small stage at 9 P.M.

CASA DEL MAR

<u>Casa del Mar Hotel, 1910 Ocean Way (at Pico), Santa Monica (310) 581-5533. Open Sun.–Thurs., 6:30 a.m.–midnight; Fri. and Sat., 6:30 a.m.–1 a.m. Full bar. 21 and over. No cover. Food (American). $$.</u>

Tropical meets Empire in the lobby of the Casa del Mar Hotel. The colossal room is tastefully outfitted with club chairs, double-wide couches, a room-size hearth, and an absolutely massive center bar. The place caters to high-end business travelers as well as children of privilege—the kind who slap "Harvard" stickers to the rear window of the Volvo (and loiter in the lobby library, thumbing through books that appear to have been chosen for girth rather than content). But never mind: such silliness is offset by the sheer comfort of the place. Seated at one of the substantial cocktail tables, nibbling little dishes of nuts and olives, with a piano tinkling just out of sight line and the sun setting over the Pacific, one feels a sloshy sense of peace and plenty, and gratitude for being able to spend a few hours in such profuse abundance. If you plan on staying longer, however, bring your platinum card: rooms start at $345.

CASA VEGA

<u>13301 Ventura Blvd. (at Fulton), Sherman Oaks (818) 788-4868. Open Mon.–Fri., 11 a.m.–2 a.m., Sat. and Sun., 4:30 p.m.–2 a.m. Full bar. All ages in dining area. No cover. Food (Mexican). $$.</u>

A friendly Mexican restaurant with a legendary Happy Hour: from 2:30 p.m. to 5:30 p.m., you will find carpenters from the studios, older Valley matrons in white gloves, party kids from over the hill, and harried moms with kids in tow all swilling strong margaritas in a room redder than a busted capillary. Festive and inexpensive, with Mex-American meals to ballast the alcohol, Casa Vega is one of the few bars in the Valley worth the trip.

CATALINA BAR AND GRILL

1640 CAHUENGA BLVD. (A HALF BLOCK SOUTH OF HOLLYWOOD), HOLLYWOOD (323) 466-2210. WWW.CATALINAJAZZCLUB.COM. OPEN SUN.–THURS., 7 P.M.–1 A.M.; FRI. AND SAT., 7 P.M.–2 A.M. FULL BAR. ALL AGES. COVER VARIES. FOOD (ITALIAN AND AMERICAN). $$$.

Hollywood's premier jazz spot, attracting big-name players and serious fans. Vaguely Eastern European decor (Catalina was opened, in 1986, by Romanian Catalina Popescu) and supper-table seating make it a grown-up spot, the sort of jazz club where one dines while listening politely to legends like Joe Williams and Betty Carter. One of the places the big names play while passing through LA. Reservations a must.

THE CAT N' FIDDLE PUB

6530 SUNSET BLVD. (BETWEEN HIGHLAND AND CAHUENGA, AT WILCOX), HOLLYWOOD (323) 468-3800. OPEN DAILY, 11:30 A.M.–2 A.M. FULL BAR. ALL AGES UNTIL 8 P.M.; 21 AND OVER AFTER. NO COVER. FOOD (BRITISH PUB). $$.

A British pub where they know how to tap a proper black and tan, bake a shepherd's pie, and generally extend pub geniality. The room is a throwback not so much to Olde England as to early 1970s Americana, with lots of stained glass and waxed wood surfaces. The inside booths are high enough to hibernate in, and the patio, sun-dappled and pretty by day, becomes a very happening scene at night, with people from all over the globe sitting and chatting and smoking and drinking. An excellent place to watch the World Cup.

CAVA

Beverly Plaza Hotel, 8384 W. 3rd St. (between La Cienega and Crescent Heights, at Orlando), LA (323) 658-8898. Open Mon.–Fri., 6:30 p.m.–11:30 a.m.; Sat. and Sun., 6:30 a.m.–12:30 p.m. Full bar. 21 and over. Cover varies. Food (Spanish). $$.

This Harlequinesque bar and supper club, upstairs at the Beverly Plaza Hotel, features all things Spanish: bands of guitar-strumming gypsies, salsa nights, flamenco shows, a "Barcelona Brunch." The rooms are color-saturated and whimsically decorated (oversize gold chandeliers, burgundy velvet banquettes), there's a tapa-laden Happy Hour starting weekdays at 4 P.M. and Spanish cuisine and entertainment every night. A lively midway-between-Eastside-and-Westside spot to meet/bring a date, it's also within walking distance from the Beverly Center.

C BAR

8442 Wilshire Blvd. (one block east of La Cienega), Beverly Hills (323) 782-8157. Open Mon.–Fri., 5:30 p.m.–2 a.m.; Sat., 6:30 p.m.–2 a.m.; Sun., 8 p.m.–2 a.m. Full bar. 21 and over (18 in dining area). No cover. Food (caviar, etc.) $$.

Good idea, good execution: this gorgeous, seductive, Deco-inspired caviar-and-cocktail bar next-door to the Wilshire Theater acts as a polestar to nearby agents, clubhoppers, couples celebrating anniversaries, and anyone who wants to pretend they're a Romanov for the evening. With etched-glass walls, a red-lacquered tin ceiling, booths made for nestling and swoony tunes (you *will* hear "The Girl from Ipanema"), C Bar is unquestionably romantic; you can't go wrong to bring a date. The cocktails are bits of whimsy (a Caiprinha, made with the Brazilian sugarcane liquor *cachaça*, arrives with a jewel-tone plastic mermaid arced suggestively over the rim), and the caviar is a theatrical production in miniature: ounces of beluga served with all the dainty accompaniments (silver-dollar-size blini, crème fraîche, minced egg yolk). Feeling more proletarian? Park yourself at the bar with a burger and a beer (or one of 50 brands of vodka), and enjoy the eroticism from afar.

CHEETAHS

4600 HOLLYWOOD BLVD. (TWO BLOCKS EAST OF VERMONT), LOS FELIZ (323) 660-6733. WWW.CHEETAHSOFHOLLYWOOD.COM. OPEN MON.–SAT., 1 P.M.–2 A.M.; SUN., 6 P.M.–2 A.M. FULL BAR. 21 AND OVER. COVER THURS.–SAT., $8. NO FOOD. $$.

Back in the seventies, any self-respecting strip club had an elevated catwalk, lots of mirrors, and a pole—preferably two. Though Cheetahs didn't open until the nineties, it cleaves to this stylistic formula. The dancers (most good-looking, about half surgically enhanced) hark from the "Flashdance" school, incorporating costumes/dramatic personae into their two-song routines, and making excellent, acrobatic use of the pole. Customers run to working Joes, local Bohos, and various strip-joint regulars. Though of course there's no touching the talent, things have been known to get rather heated at Cheetahs around closing time. At least, I'm pretty sure I saw my friend Trixie French-kissing a dancer named Flame.

CHERRY. *See listing under "Playroom."*

CHEZ JAY

1657 OCEAN AVE. (SOUTH OF COLORADO), SANTA MONICA (310) 395-1741. WWW.CHEZJAYS.COM. OPEN DAILY, 11:30 A.M.–

1:30 P.M. FULL BAR. ALL AGES. NO COVER. FOOD (SEAFOOD). $$.

Tiny seaside shanty with a porthole in the front door and some really nice folks inside, including owner Jay Fiondella, who opened the place in 1959 and who now runs it with wife Lucy. It's important that you know their names, because they'll want to know yours, in order to make you feel at home. The minute you walk in, you understand this is the sort of place, body willing, you will always return to—a universal sentiment judging by the cadre of old salts bellied up to the twinkle-lit bar. Don't feel like drinking? Grab a booth (try to nab the big, ultraprivate one in back) and order the sautéed sand dabs, which come, should you accept the challenge, with a house specialty: potatoes mashed with bananas.

CINEGRILL CABARET AND LOUNGE

HOLLYWOOD ROOSEVELT HOTEL, 7000 HOLLYWOOD BLVD. (ONE BLOCK EAST OF HIGHLAND) (323) 466-7000. OPEN NIGHTLY, 8 P.M.–2 A.M. FULL BAR, 21 AND OVER. COVER VARIES. FOOD (APPETIZERS AND BAR SNACKS). $$.

Every time I read about Cinegrill, the intimate cabaret off the lobby of the Hollywood Roosevelt Hotel, it's referred to either as legendary (because 60-plus years ago Hemingway and Fitzgerald drank here, but where didn't they drink?) or historic (the Hollywood Roosevelt being the original home of the Oscars). Neither of these appellatives entices me enough to make me go to Cinegrill, which, in its present incarnation, resembles what it is—a hotel bar with loud carpeting (don't look down if you've had one too many), conditioned air, and a good number of tourists. And yet there is a very good and currently legitimate reason to venerate Cinegrill, and that is its impeccable booking policy, which features true legends like Eartha Kitt as well as Broadway performers, jazz greats, and lounge acts. The crowd tends to be mellow—a chummy theatrical community that supports live local music.

CINNABAR

933 S. BRAND BLVD. (ONE BLOCK NORTH OF CHEVY CHASE), GLENDALE (818) 551-1155. OPEN SUN.–THURS., 6 P.M.–11 P.M., FRI. AND SAT., 6 P.M.–MIDNIGHT. FULL BAR. ALL AGES. NO COVER. FOOD (ECLECTIC). $$.

Everyone I know loves Cinnabar—The Little Bar That Could—despite its seating only about ten (there's a larger dining area in the back) and its no-zone location, where it is dwarfed by the dozens of auto dealerships on Brand Boulevard. Never mind; it's worth a trip, as the bar itself is stunning—a carved-ivory shrine salvaged from a defunct Chinatown bar called Yee Mee Lu's and depicting a holy pilgrimage. The music's always sweet and seductive (there's the occasional piano player and vocalist), the bartenders are interesting, and the drinks are quirky and good (try an icy Moscow Mule). A vivid, tucked-away spot in which to spend an evening.

CIRCLE BAR

2926 MAIN ST. (BETWEEN ROSE AND OCEAN PARK), SANTA MONICA (310) 450-0508. OPEN NIGHTLY, 5 P.M.–2 A.M. FULL BAR. 21 AND OVER. NO COVER. NO FOOD. $$.

Back in the early nineties, lounges such as Jones and Good Luck went the black lacquer/moody-red-lighting route, ushering in the return of the lush life. Circle Bar must've gotten wind of it in 1999, when they turned what had for decades been a beery kids' bar into Santa Monica's only lounge approximation, with a good mix-and-mingle scene, funky piped-in tunes, and a triptych of Bruce Lee in action on the back wall. The effort's appreciated; as my friend Monica says, "It's the only place around here that's not full of Dockers frat boys or the annoying ponytail producer crowd." Local hipsters, barely distinguishable from their Hollywood cousins, pack the place every night, thrilled to slake their thirsts in their own area code. (Though not without a price: a glass of wine runs $7.)

CLUB 7969/PEANUTS

7969 Santa Monica Blvd. (one block west of Fairfax), West Hollywood (323) 654-0280. Open nightly, 9 p.m.–2 a.m. Full bar. 21 and over; some clubs, 18 and over. Cover, $6–$10. No food. $$.

Who wants to go to a bar called Peanuts? You do, if any part of you is interested in venues where sex/stripping/S and M are the order of the evening. Every night's a different scene, including the long-running **Michelle's XXX Topless Revue** (Tuesday), a supertheatrical female-strip show/dance club that attracts as many gals as guys; **Sin-A-Matic** (Saturday), which promotes itself as "LA's premier fetish club" and offers the bondage-wear set erotic videos, psychotropic house music, and a spanking room; and **Vibrator** (Thursday), the social equivalent of four raunchy hours spent with your battery-operated buddy, with deejays spinning glam, metal and punk, go-go guys and gals gyrating in as little as the law allows, and a special performance each week.

CLUB TEE YEE

3210 Glendale Blvd. (one block north of Glenhurst), Atwater Village (323) 669-9631. Open daily, 9 a.m.–2 a.m. Full bar. 21 and over. No cover. No food. $.

You won't know about Tee Yee unless you live down the block, or used to, as I did. Tee Yee is a little out-of-the-way (Atwater Village), and the big barn of a room has zero decoration. The place is Anybar, USA: quiet, with a jukebox that tends toward beer-crying tunes by Freddie Fender and Al Martino, and locals who don't mind if you hang out there on a Saturday night but aren't impressed that you do. One plus: there's always an open stool. One minus: sometimes it's not open when it's supposed to be.

THE COACH & HORSES

7617 SUNSET BLVD. (BETWEEN FAIRFAX AND LA BREA, AT STANLEY), WEST HOLLYWOOD (323) 876-6900. OPEN DAILY, NOON–2 A.M. FULL BAR. 21 AND OVER. NO COVER. NO FOOD. $.

Though the sconces in the entryway make it look as though you're about to enter a Ye Olde English pub, inside is an American dive. Centrally located, the Coach & Horses is inexpensive and friendly—the sort of place where you and a friend stop for a quick beer or where, on those gray days, you sit by yourself for hours, which you are at liberty to do, since, as far as I can tell, The Coach & Horses' period as a frat-boy hang ended around 1997. Not a destination, but a worthy stop on the bar tour.

COCONUT CLUB

BEVERLY HILTON HOTEL, 9876 WILSHIRE BLVD. (AT SANTA MONICA), BEVERLY HILLS (310) 285-1358. WWW.MERV.COM/COCONUTCLUB. OPEN FRI. AND SAT. ONLY, 7:30 P.M.–2 A.M. FULL BAR. 21 AND OVER. $10 COVER. FOOD (CAL-ECLECTIC). $$$.

It's a Merv, Merv, Mervelous world when you log onto merv.com and check out the Griffin dynasty of game shows and luxury resorts, TV shows like *Men Are from Mars*,

Women Are from Venus, and CDs like Merv's *It's Like a Dream.* A spin around Merv's virtual world is surely more fun than actually going to the Coconut Club, located in Merv Griffin's Beverly Hills Hotel (yes, that's the official name). The Club is a huge ballroom with silver and gold palm trees, pink and purple lighting, sugary drinks overspilling fruit, and a cigar room called Chimp's—in other words, a game show in the form of a club, which may delight the guests upstairs, but which can cause vertigo and/or an emotional meltdown in those not quite used to the sweet stuff. Live music, mostly swing and big band, with complimentary dance lessons.

COCONUT TEASZER

8117 SUNSET BLVD. (A HALF BLOCK WEST OF CRESCENT HEIGHTS), WEST HOLLYWOOD (323) 654-4773. OPEN NIGHTLY, 8 P.M.–2 A.M. FULL BAR. 18 AND OVER, EXCEPT MON. AND TUES., 21 AND OVER. COVER VARIES. FOOD (FRI. AND SAT. ONLY, TACOS AND BURGERS). $$.

A cozy, dark club with a little more edge/humor than neighboring rock venues, and a place appreciated by scores of fledgling musicians, who've taken advantage of the Teaszer's (and manager-booker Len Fagan's) policy of giving new-to-town bands a stage on which to play. Six ready-to-rock groups a night, and a crowd that spends a lot of time on their hair, especially the girlies, who appear to have pledged fealty to seventies glitz and/or the mid-eighties club-slut look. Hey, I'm not complaining. Also site of the after-hours club **Does Your Mama Know?** (Sunday, 3 P.M. to 9 A.M.), with diehards dancing to deejay Tony Largo's hard-driving house and sucking down fruit juice 'til the bar reopens at 6 A.M.

THE CONGA ROOM

5364 WILSHIRE BLVD. (TWO BLOCKS WEST OF LA BREA), MIRACLE MILE (323) 938-1696. WWW.CONGAROOM.COM. OPEN WED.-SAT., 10 P.M.-2 A.M.; CLOSED SUN.-TUES. FULL BAR. 21 AND OVER. COVER VARIES, $10-45. FOOD (CUBAN). $$$.

I was skeptical when I attended the opening for this massive club, a former Jack LaLanne health spa turned superswank mecca for Latin music. My reasoning went: how (and why) were all these Westside, Armani-wearing, uptight agent types going to abandon themselves to the freeform arrhythmia of Latin music? But then Jimmy Smits (one of the celebrity backers, along with Jennifer Lopez and Paul Rodriguez) asked me to dance, and my brain turned to guava jelly. As the lights reflected off the mirror balls, and as Tito Puente and his band blared what sounded like a thousand horns, I surrendered. I love the Conga Room. I love the minty *mojitos*, love sneaking into the VIP cigar lounge to flirt with guys holding stogies between their teeth, love watching the ultrasharp dancers burn holes in the floor. And I am not the only one: thanks to a great booking policy and the addition of a Cuban restaurant, La Boca, the Conga Room has not only stood the test of time but has flourished. What did I know?

COWBOY PALACE SALOON

21635 DEVONSHIRE ST. (AT OWENSMOUTH), CHATSWORTH (818) 341-0166. OPEN MON.-FRI., 2 P.M.-2 A.M.; SAT., 3 P.M.-2 A.M.; SUN., 3 P.M.-MIDNIGHT. FULL BAR. 21 AND OVER. NO COVER. NO REGULAR FOOD SERVICE, BUT SEE BELOW. $$.

This great big dance hall/bar bills itself as "the Last Real Honky Tonk." There are cowboy boots dangling from the ceiling and an American flag hanging over the stage, and the place is full of real cowboys and cowgirls and those who'd like to be. Superfriendly scene. Don't know how to two-step? Heck, that guy with the bronc on his belt buckle'll help you, or you can follow the dance instructors, who hold classes for free every evening starting at 6:30. There's a complimentary barbecue on Sunday and a Monday Hungry Hour. All this, and live shit-kicking music every night of the week. It may be off the beaten track, but if you're hankering for country, it's worth the trip.

CRAZY GIRLS

1433 N. LA BREA AVE. (AT SUNSET), HOLLYWOOD (323) 969-0055. OPEN NIGHTLY, 7 P.M.–2 A.M. FULL BAR. 21 AND OVER. COVER, $5. NO FOOD. $$.

The strippers at Crazy Girls are perfect—every ounce of leg-and-buttock flesh loofahed/lipoed to superlative tautness. Breasts are either so pert they appear in danger of choking their owner, or so expensively sculpted they obediently stay in place even when the girls are dangling upside down, contorting into pretzel shapes, or panting on all fours for an overwhelmingly male audience so distracted they don't seem to notice or much care they're paying $8 per drink. The room itself must have 100,000 mirrors, with ray gun lighting and earsplitting rock designed to create a strip experience in Sensurround. If you like your topless girls with all the trimmings, this is the place.

THE CRUSH BAR

1735 CAHUENGA BLVD. (ONE BLOCK NORTH OF HOLLYWOOD), HOLLYWOOD (323) 461-9017. OPEN FRI. AND SAT., 9 P.M.–7 A.M.; THURS. NIGHT/FRI. MORNING, 2:30 A.M.–7 A.M.; CLOSED. MON.–THURS. FULL BAR. 21 AND OVER. COVER, $10. NO FOOD. $$.

An oldie but goodie, the Crush Bar is a big rambling dance club where they play the sort of sixties Motown and seventies pop songs everyone can sing in their sleep. While there's nothing hip about the Crush Bar, it's certainly reliable and comfortably corny, a good spot to bring in-laws from, say, Okmulgee, Oklahoma (which I did and everyone had a blast). The Crush Bar hosts after-hours dance clubs Thursday through Saturday, 2:30 A.M. to 7 A.M.

THE CULVER SALOON

11513 WASHINGTON BLVD. (SIX BLOCKS WEST OF SEPULVEDA), CULVER CITY (310) 391-1519. OPEN TUES.–SAT., 7 P.M.–2 A.M.; FRI., 4 P.M.–2 A.M.; CLOSED SUN. AND MON. FULL BAR. 21 AND OVER. COVER VARIES. NO FOOD. $$.

There are live country, rockabilly, and blues bands six nights a week in this Western honky-tonk with a great booking policy that brings in acts from Big Sandy and His Fly-Rite Boys to Candye Kane. Friendly folks, two pool tables, a great big dance floor flooded with fantasy lighting, and a scene that gets boisterous as the night goes on. Hollering? Chit, yeah. Line-dancing? Hell, yes, and free lessons to boot. Go with a group, drink a bunch of beer, and dance yourself into a sweaty mess.

DADDY'S

1610 N. VINE ST. (BETWEEN SUNSET AND HOLLYWOOD, AT SELMA), HOLLYWOOD (323) 463-7777. OPEN MON.–SAT., 8 P.M.–2 A.M.; SUN., 9 P.M.–2 A.M. FULL BAR. 21 AND OVER. NO COVER. NO FOOD. $$.

After two years in business, Lucky Seven, a stylish supper club with a cool forties decor, was completely revamped as Daddy's. Gone sea-foam lighting; in throbbing red. Out big steak dinners while luxuriating in high back booths; in rolling ottomans and low tables, on and around which hipsters drink and laugh and woo. Luckily, the beautiful bar remains, as do the swell bartenders and an easy lounge ambiance that bids one to sit for hours. Well done both ways; one of Hollywood's choicer spots.

DAMON'S STEAK HOUSE

317 N. BRAND BLVD. (BETWEEN LEXINGTON AND CALIFORNIA), GLENDALE (818) 507-1510. OPEN SUN.–THURS., 9 A.M.–10 P.M., FRI. AND SAT., 9 A.M.–11:30 P.M. FULL BAR. ALL AGES. NO COVER. FOOD (STEAKS). $$.

Why did someone open a Tiki-themed steakhouse in Glendale in the 1930s? Because they had a generous heart, and understood that, if you give people a good (though by no means gourmet) steak, a large chopped salad, and a pile of greasy garlic bread for a ridiculously reasonable price, you will win customers for life. And Damon's has: with its thatched-grass ceilings and 1940s murals of barely dressed Pacific Islanders, Damon's is home to everyone—retirees and families, locals and lushes—who has discovered the $3 *mai tai*s are sweet and strong and go down much too easy. Bring the kids; Damon's doesn't mind if they scoot between tables and press their noses to the massive tank of tropical fish, allowing Mom and Dad to linger over dinner and drinks, content that there are still a few places like Damon's around.

DEEP

1707 N. VINE ST. (CORNER OF HOLLYWOOD BLVD.), HOLLYWOOD (323) 462-1144. OPEN TUES.–SAT., 7 P.M.–2 A.M. FULL BAR. COVER, $10 THURSDAY, $15 FRIDAY AND SATURDAY. 21 AND OVER. FOOD (AMERICAN). $$.

Deep, as in inside the body, is the design scheme behind Ivan Kane's new bar and restaurant on the legendary corner of Hollywood and Vine. And a lush and labyrinthine journey it is, starting with the deeply-red main bar, whose rear windows-of-pleasure showcase barely-clad dancers performing **Fosse-esque** moves. Want to go deeper? Head for the back bar, purple and silver and black-lit, and enter the large Plexiglas cube that serves as a dance floor. Look up, and watch three dancers—two female, one male—performing risqué routines on a platform overhead, or watch yourself, in the two-way mirrored walls, while people outside the cube look at you. Deeper still? Rent one of the large walk-in coolers that have been transformed into VIP party rooms, where, for a grand or so, you and fifteen of your friends can have your own bartender and dancer. Food is intended to get/keep you in the mood (oysters, gravlax, filet, chocolate fondue). Sound good? Everyone else thinks so, too, which means you may or may not get past the door guy on weekends.

THE DERBY

4500 LOS FELIZ BLVD. (AT HILLHURST), LOS FELIZ (323) 663-8979. WWW.THE-DERBY.COM. OPEN DAILY, 4 P.M.–2 A.M. FULL BAR. 21 AND OVER. COVER VARIES. FOOD (ITALIAN AND AMERICAN, FROM LOUISE'S NEXT DOOR). $$.

Back in the early nineties, the Derby picked up on the swing revival bigger and better than any other place in town. A massive room with a huge horseshoe-shaped bar (modeled after the one in the film *Mildred Pierce*), a real (if small) dance floor, and red-hot big bands every night of the week, whoo-doggie, the Derby was happening. Then they filmed *Swingers* here. Suddenly *everybody* came. Then everybody who'd hopped on swing as a trend left. And yet the Derby is still packed. A recent night there shows no sign that this truly beautiful, forties-evocative venue is slowing down; if anything, it's even more exhilarating. The music blasts you right down to your socks, and the dancers are so hot that those of us who don't East Coast swing, jitterbug, and/or lindy-hop can only watch in awe, go into the other room to practice, or take lessons (they're offered every night, and they're free). A big, brash eyeful of a place, even if you just watch the horn section. Great place to bring out of town visitors.

DOMINICK'S

8715 BEVERLY BLVD. (BETWEEN SAN VINCENTE AND ROBERTSON), LA (310) 652-7272. OPEN MON.-THUR., 7 P.M.-12:30 A.M.; FRI. AND SAT., 7 P.M.-2 A.M.; CLOSED SUN. FULL BAR. ALL AGES. NO COVER. FOOD (STEAKS). $$$.

The adage "If you build it, they will come" has never been truer than for Jon Sidel, former mastermind behind some of LA's best-loved and long-gone scenes (Power Tools, the Olive, Small's K.O.). Several years ago, Sidel transformed a haunt once owned by Sinatra and frequented by the Rat Pack into this superswank steak joint that resembles the inside of a sumptuous yacht. And come they have—not just club kids familiar with Sidel's Midas touch, but everyone who appreciates a great martini and a perfect steak: cadres of ladies in St. John knits, development executives working their Palm Pilots, and, on the very pretty patio, models and their ilk basking in the glow of a huge stone fireplace and their own beauty. If you're into the scene, by all means; if your taste runs to a triumphant New York strip, even better.

DRAGONFLY

6510 Santa Monica Blvd. (between Highland and Cahuenga, at Wilcox), Hollywood (323) 466-6111. www.dragonfly.com. Open nightly, 9 p.m.–2 a.m., with occasional early shows starting at 7 p.m. Full bar. 21 and over. Cover $5–$15. No food. $$.

Dragonfly has always been a very heated scene, with a Casbah/death rocker motif, a big patio, the occasional big name dropping in to gig, and an adventurous booking policy (funk, rock, reggae, punk, hip-hop). But its popularity has spiked these past few years, in part due to the **Pretty Ugly Club** (Wednesday), where angry young men rage and all the girlies, dressed to thrill, make for an eye-popping mix. Dragonfly attracts the sort of freaky, nonstop crowd that knows what's going on, where and on which night, and chooses to spend a lot of those nights here. Take it or leave it: a 28-year-old friend who used to hang at Dragonfly every night says she can't go anymore because she feels too old.

THE DRAWING ROOM

1800 Hillhurst Ave. (two blocks south of Franklin), Los Feliz (323) 665-0135. Open daily, 6 a.m.–2 a.m. Full bar. 21 and over. No cover. No food. $.

This local bar mixes newer Los Feliz denizens—hipsters, artists, film folks—with the regular drinkers who've kept this place in business for years. And a colorful group these regulars are; don't be surprised if you find yourself in a tape-loop conversation with a guy with a gin-blossomed nose or an oddly shaped head. Ambiance is Basic Bar: cheap drinks, a big TV, a few video games. Though finding a place to sit here on a Saturday is becoming harder and harder, I find myself cleaving to the romantic notion that, no matter how packed, the Drawing Room will always remain a local dive.

DRESDEN ROOM

1760 N. VERMONT AVE. (BETWEEN FRANKLIN AND HOLLYWOOD), LOS FELIZ (323) 665-4294. OPEN DAILY, 10 A.M.–2 A.M. FULL BAR. 21 AND OVER IN BAR. NO COVER. FOOD (AMERICAN). $$.

If you haven't yet been to the Dresden, go, if only to experience the Marty and Elayne phenomenon. This vaguely vampiric (white-white skin, black-black hair, matching overbites) husband-and-wife team have been singing basically the same set in the same fabulous polyester lounge outfits for over 20 years, wowing generations with their versions of "Muskrat Love" and "Up, Up and Away." While some people find them embarrassing, others simply thrill, and all agree Marty and Elayne are inimitable. And yet the Dresden is about more than the floor show: the room is a sweeping, high-ceilinged affair that puts one in mind of a Scandinavian ski lodge, and the bar is gorgeous, a great place for a cocktail in the afternoon (when the place is empty). By night, the crowd is a real mixed bag: old gents, college kids, lots of Europeans. And then there's the dining room, a place where I always expect to find the ghosts of Liberace and/or some Gabor sisters: undulating columns, gold accents everywhere, high-back white leather booths that beg to be draped with a silver fox cape. Invite someone to lunch here—he or she will be thrilled.

DUBLIN'S PUB

8240 SUNSET BLVD. (TWO BLOCKS WEST OF CRESCENT HEIGHTS), SUNSET STRIP (323) 656-0100. OPEN MON.-FRI.,

11 A.M.–2 A.M.; SAT. AND SUN., 10 A.M.–2 A.M. FULL BAR. 21 AND OVER. NO COVER. FOOD (IRISH PUB). $$.

Dine upstairs, drink downstairs, or play pool and watch the game with young, brash Hollywood hopefuls downing Harp and generally feeling their oats. Large, loud, and frat-boy heavy, Dublin's is more suggestive of Boston than of LA. Everyone's main gripes: the parking, like that of every other place in the area, is a nightmare, and the inanity of being made to wait 45 minutes (also known as Sunset Strip hospitality) in order to drink in an Irish pub. Unless you're into snotty boys/the starlet thing, I'd give Dublin's the shine.

EL CARMEN

8138 W. 3RD ST. (ONE BLOCK WEST OF CRESCENT HEIGHTS), LA (323) 852-1556. OPEN SUN.–THURS., 5 P.M.–2 A.M., FRI. AND SAT., 7 P.M.–2 A.M. FULL BAR. 21 AND OVER. NO COVER. FOOD (MEXICAN). $$.

The latest from LA scenemaster Sean McPherson, El Carmen is smashing. The walls are saturated with color, from the 1947 oil portraits of the masked Mexican wrestlers known as Los Luchadores to the hundreds of small Technicolor posters lining the walls. And what liquor! Over 100 tequilas and 25 mescals (many of the latter imported from tiny villages around Oaxaca), which in terms of effect fall somewhere between alcohol and a hallucinogen (as you will most keenly notice after you've fallen asleep, when you wind up in the Dreamland of the Demented). The only problem with El Carmen, which I love, is that everyone else loves it, too, which makes it a tight squeeze on the weekends.

EL CHAVO

4441 SUNSET BLVD. (AT SUNSET DR.), SILVERLAKE (323) 664-0871. OPEN SUN.–THURS., 11:30 A.M.–10 P.M.; SAT. AND SUN., 11:30 A.M.–11:00 P.M. FULL BAR. 21 AND OVER IN THE BAR. NO COVER. FOOD (MEXICAN). $.

This family-friendly Mexican restaurant has a tiny bar on one side, a sweet hideaway lit by twinkle lights, with colorful sombreros adorning the ceiling and a few too many photos of Dolly Parton on the wall. "Oh, she comes here a lot," says owner Ricardo de la Garza, a perennial bachelor in a Ban-Lon shirt and pointy white boots. "And last night, we have Barry White with a party of ten." Is any of this true? If Parton and White are smart, it is. El Chavo is perfectly pitched between vibrant and tranquil—the concept of the perfect little Mexican bar made manifest. And the icy margaritas are divine.

EL CID

4212 SUNSET BLVD. (FIVE BLOCKS EAST OF VERMONT), SILVERLAKE (323) 668-0318. WWW.ELCID-CA.COM. OPEN WED.–SUN., 6:30 P.M.–2 A.M.; CLOSED MON. AND TUES. FULL BAR. ALL AGES. COVER VARIES. FOOD (SPANISH). $$.

A 40-year-old Spanish *taverna* with nightly flamenco shows, El Cid boasts a big red and gold sign that is a landmark on this barren stretch of east Sunset in Silverlake. Situated below street level, the club is as austere and dramatic as an El Greco. Sit in the little bar in back, or at a supper table facing the stage, and watch flamenco dancers, including the occasional international star, perform up to three shows per night. On Sunday, there's a champagne brunch accompanied by a big band made up of women musicians who've been playing swing since the forties. An unusual, quietly glamorous spot, and the only place of its kind in LA.

EL COMPADRE

7408 W. SUNSET BLVD. (BETWEEN LA BREA AND FAIRFAX, AT VISTA), WEST HOLLYWOOD (323) 874-7924. OPEN DAILY, 11:30 A.M.–2 A.M. FULL BAR. 21 AND OVER IN BAR; ALL AGES IN RESTAURANT. NO COVER. FOOD (MEXICAN). $.

Tucked along one end of this old-school, family-run Mexican restaurant is a grotto of a bar, serving bland chips and cheap, sweet margaritas to a mostly local WeHo crowd. Dark as a cave, El Compadre is a cool, calm place to hibernate on a hot afternoon; if you're still there come evening (with not one peep of natural light, you'll know it's past 6 P.M. when the mariachi band begins to play), slide into one of the U-shaped vinyl booths and enjoy a basic one-platter, smothered-in-white-cheese Mexican combo.

EL COYOTE

7312 BEVERLY BLVD. (BETWEEN FAIRFAX AND LA BREA, AT MARTEL), LOS ANGELES (323) 939-2255. OPEN SUN.–THURS., 11 A.M.–10 P.M.; FRI. AND SAT., 11 A.M.–11 P.M. FULL BAR. ALL AGES. NO COVER. FOOD (MEXICAN). $.

This 65-year-old Mexican restaurant, a labyrinth of rooms and bars and patios, is saturated in color, from the fiesta decorations to the dizzying flounces on the waitresses' skirts. While the food is not very good—everything you order comes covered in cheese and oozing orange oil—the margaritas are legendary, truly delicious, and incredibly cheap. I like El Coyote in the late afternoon, before the hordes of families and tourists and USC/UCLA students arrive. Yet even when it's packed, the layout and lighting of the place is campy and magical. A good place to bring a group.

EL FLORIDITA

1253 N. VINE ST. (AT FOUNTAIN), HOLLYWOOD (323) 871-8612. OPEN SUN., TUES., THURS., 11:30 A.M.–10 P.M.; MON., WED., FRI. AND SAT., 11:30 A.M.–1 A.M. 21 AND OVER. COVER VARIES. FOOD (CUBAN). $$.

The outside gives away nothing. A Cuban restaurant in a mini-mall, right? Ha. Open the door, and you enter a world of crushed red velvet and gold, eleven-piece salsa orchestras, flared skirts and Panama hats, and a sexy little bar serving fresh *mojitos*, all vibrantly coexisting in a space no larger than a good-sized living-room. El Floridita is an excellent destination Monday nights, when Johnny Polanco y Su Conjunto Amistad blare their New York salsa for an adoring crowd, who, between bites of garlicky pork and fried plantains, burn up the teeny dance floor. Always a hit, and an exhilarating surprise for people who think they're just stepping out for a bite.

EL REY THEATER

5515 WILSHIRE BLVD. (BETWEEN LA BREA AND FAIRFAX, CORNER OF BURNSIDE), MIRACLE MILE (323) 936-4790. HOURS VARY. FULL BAR. 18 AND OVER. COVER VARIES. NO FOOD. $$.

Most often a concert venue, the Deco-inspired, slightly tatty El Rey Theater also hosts the obscenely popular **Make-Up** (first Saturday of every month; for more information: (323) 796-5500, www.clubmakeup.net). "A Glitter Extravaganza!" put on by deejays/promoters Jason Lavitt and Joseph Brooks, Make-Up marries glam rock, live performance, and lavish midnight drag shows, and draws a fervent, glammed-to-the-max, pansexual crowd that can reach into the thousands. You read that right, baby, so get there early if you want to get in, because even the enormous El Rey cannot accommodate this number without the fire marshal getting his hose in a knot.

ENCOUNTER

LOS ANGELES INTERNATIONAL AIRPORT, 201 WORLD WAY, WESTCHESTER (310) 215-5151. OPEN SUN.–THURS., 11 A.M.–11 P.M.; FRI. AND SAT., 11 A.M.–12:30 A.M. ALL AGES IN RESTAURANT; 21 AND OVER AT THE BAR. NO COVER. FOOD ("CONTINENTAL CUISINE"). $$.

The next time your plane is delayed, don't wander between the newsstand and the depressing airport bar. Instead, head over to the Theme Building, that futuristic structure with the parabolic arches, which is the site of the restaurant and lounge Encounter. Billed as "Space Age Dining and Drinking for the Jet Set," Encounter bases its look on The Future! as designers rendered it in the sixties—all curves/no angles, low-to-the-ground seating (safer for takeoff), and beams of purple light. Music is usually Bachelor Pad (e.g., Esquivel, Mancini, Bossa Nova), though it becomes friskier on Friday, when deejay Señor Amor spins a sex-driven seventies set, from Queen Donna Summer and King Barry White on down.

FAIS DO-DO

5257 W. ADAMS BLVD. (BETWEEN LA BREA AND FAIRFAX, AT CLOVERDALE), LA (323) 954-8080. WWW.FAISDODO.COM. USUALLY OPEN WED.–SUN., 7 P.M.–2 A.M. ALL AGES. COVER USUALLY $5. FOOD (CAJUN-CALIFORNIA). $$.

Situated in the middle of nowhere in what was once a squat and stately bank, Fais Do-Do does what most clubs in the high-rent districts do not have the luxury to do: anything it wants. Cajun and Zydeco, comedy and theater, funk and film screenings, soul and English disco—you name it, they do it, while serving up pretty good Cajun chow and a major selection of micro-brews. The crowd is always a pleasure: interesting, wry, ready. Bring a slew of smart people looking for something new.

FARMER'S MARKET BARS—EB'S AND 326

CORNER OF 3RD ST. AND FAIRFAX AVE., LA (323) 933-9211. WWW.FARMERSMARKETBARS.COM. MARKET IS OPEN MON.–SAT., 9 A.M.–7 P.M.; SUN., 10 A.M.–6 P.M.; BARS OPEN SLIGHTLY LATER. BEER AND WINE ONLY. ALL AGES. NO COVER. FOOD (ALL KINDS AVAILABLE IN THE MARKET). $.

The Third Place is a British expression meaning the location where a writer goes, apart from home and work, to sit and cogitate. Usually it's a bar; in LA, it's the Farmer's Market, that collision of cuisine and tourism and literary woolgathering. The Farmer's Market also has two pubs where there is karaoke most Saturdays from 6:30 P.M. to 9:30 P.M. The pubs are EB's (the larger bar in the center of the Market) and 326 (the no-more-than-a-zinc-counter flush against the Market's west wall), where, as humanity ambles past with jambalaya and crêpes, candy apples and manicotti, you can drink good British ale and sing words someone else wrote.

FATHER'S OFFICE

1018 MONTANA AVE. (AT 10TH ST.), SANTA MONICA (310) 393-2337. OPEN MON.–THURS., 5 P.M.–2 A.M.; FRI.–SUN., 4 P.M.–2 A.M. BEER AND WINE ONLY. 21 AND OVER. NO COVER. NO FOOD. $.

Nice, bright beer bar with over 30 micro-brews and a cache of periodicals and board games scattered across the tables to keep you busy. Friendly local clientele make it a good neighborhood spot for a beer and a game of backgammon, or a comfortable place to spend the evening reading and sipping. Easy to find: follow the old-time neon arrow pointing the way.

FENIX BAR

ARGYLE HOTEL, 8358 SUNSET BLVD. (TWO BLOCKS EAST OF LA CIENEGA), WEST HOLLYWOOD (323) 848-6677. OPEN DAILY, 11 A.M.–2 A.M. FULL BAR. 21 AND OVER. NO COVER. FOOD (CAL-ECLECTIC). $$.

The Fenix Bar, located in the very beautiful, Deco-refurbished Argyle Hotel, exemplifies one of the images LA takes pains to exhibit, that of pampered and idle beauty. The pool/bar scene from *The Player* was filmed at the Argyle, and Hollywood's *jeunesse dorée* (DiCaprio, Damon, Paltrow) have reveled on the large, comfortable patio lit by palm-tree-shaped lamps from the twenties, enjoying cocktails, a balmy breeze, a city view, and the spoils of celebrity. If you feel like basking in a little of this brilliant if evanescent shine (and you're here, so why not?), Fenix is the best of the Strip's hotel bars at which to do so.

FIREHOUSE

213 ROSE AVE. (AT MAIN), VENICE (310) 396-6810. OPEN MON.–FRI., 7 A.M.–11 P.M.; SAT. AND SUN., 8 A.M.–11 P.M. FULL BAR. ALL AGES. NO COVER. FOOD (AMERICAN). $.

While my friend Amy Alkon swears this place is full of "FBI agents, surfers, and gym rats," the most conspicuous by far are the last, who come here after sessions at the local gyms, to power down "Four Eggs Plus Whole Chicken" options, big salads, and haystacks of pasta. While the adjoining bar scene is not really about the drinks (unless, of course, they've got a lot of carbs), after 10 P.M. Firehouse does get its share of college beer drinkers and others looking for a Venice bar where they can get through the door.

FORMOSA CAFÉ

7156 SANTA MONICA BLVD. (TWO BLOCKS WEST OF LA BREA, AT FORMOSA), WEST HOLLYWOOD (323) 850-9050. OPEN DAILY, 4 P.M.–2 A.M. FULL BAR. 21 AND OVER. NO COVER. FOOD (CHINESE-AMERICAN). $.

In 1991, when Warner Bros. Hollywood threatened to raze this restaurant and bar located in a railcar, generations of tipplers put down their drinks and raised their fists in protest, and the Formosa remained standing. The Formosa did not, however, take the corporate threat as a sign they needed to get with the times, and little appears to have changed since it first opened in 1929. The light is still barroom-dim (a blessing in the afternoon, when you are hiding from sun-bleached Santa Monica Boulevard), the walls are still lined with eight-by-ten glossies, the seating's still snug (hey, it's a railcar), and the Chinese food is still unchallenging. Though there is a new smoking patio (with big booths though little in the way of decor), the patrons, too, remain the same: hipsters young and old, and a hoary cache of screenwriters, who no doubt take smirking satisfaction that the Formosa was the site of the Lana Turner scene in *LA Confidential*, a film produced by Warner Bros.

FOUR SEASONS WINDOWS LOUNGE

FOUR SEASONS HOTEL, 300 S. DOHENY DR. (AT BURTON WAY), BEVERLY HILLS (310) 273-2222. OPEN SUN.–THURS., 11 A.M.–12:30 A.M.; FRI. AND SAT., 11 A.M.–1:30 A.M. ALL AGES. NO COVER. FOOD (CAL-ECLECTIC). $$$.

I make a point of coming here several times a year, always to meet a lady friend, and always in the late afternoon. I arrive early, so that I may sit at the bar, more often than not next to a serious gentleman who, by the way he stares straight ahead, lets me know it's cocktail time, not chatting time. With our drinks, we silently share little dishes of Niçoise olives and salted almonds. When my guest arrives, she and I adjourn to an overstuffed couch set before a fireplace and order some caviar, or perhaps the sushi-and-sashimi platter, and while we're at it, a Valentino (a marble-green vodka martini with a splash of Midori). Then I sit back and observe the parade of couture, particularly the septuagenarian goldbug goddesses and the younger women who aspire to be them, and I think, ah, the splendid efficacy of Beverly Hills.

FRANK N HANK'S

518 S. WESTERN AVE. (BETWEEN 5TH ST. AND 6TH ST.), KOREATOWN (213) 383-2087. OPEN MON.–FRI., 2 P.M.–2 A.M.; SAT. AND SUN., NOON–2 A.M. FULL BAR. 21 AND OVER. NO COVER. NO FOOD. $.

Because Koreatown has so far resisted gentrification, Frank N Hank's has had the liberty to remain what it is: a blue-collar drinking man's bar where you can always find an open stool and a clientele who, depending on your needs, will/will not make small talk. While I don't go to Frank N Hank's to meet people—we usually stop in on a weekend evening, when we're sure every place else will be packed to the gills—I have been surprised at the people who find this tiny place: one Friday, we shared the bar with two couples in their sixties who'd been drinking together/fussing at each other for 40 years, three day laborers, a tree surgeon, and a documentary filmmaker just back from Borneo. Worth a stop.

FROLIC ROOM

6245 Hollywood Blvd. (at Vine), Hollywood (323) 462-5890. Open daily, noon–2 a.m. Full bar. 21 and over. No cover. No food. $.

Smack in the heart of Hollywood, and fronted by a swooping neon sign straight out of the thirties, the Frolic Room was for a long time one of my favorites. Alas, a few years ago they started cranking the music so loud you couldn't hear what anyone said, tossed a bunch of liquor distributor freebies on the walls, and became so overrun one could barely get in the door. And yet, that sign is so heartrending, it keeps drawing us in, especially in the late afternoon, when the Frolic delivers everything a local dive should: cheap drinks, deep-dark lighting, and a client base that runs from moldy to fresh: old ladies with rouge caked in their wrinkles and kids just off the bus, the shifty eyed and the slow. In short, the people who've kept and will keep the Hollywood dream-machine rolling.

GABAH

4658 Melrose Ave. (one block west of Normandie), LA (323) 664-8913. Open nightly, 9 p.m.–2 a.m. Full bar. 21 and over. Cover, $3–$5. Food (snacks). $$.

Acid jazz, Latin beat, British pop, rhythm and blues, lots of rock—you name it, Gabah's got it on their weekly lineup of live music. The room isn't fancy (Gabah is the site of the former Anti-Club), but it has what you need: a patio, a pool table, a few snacks, a good sound system. The crowd leans toward young and arty—happy to check out four bands they've never heard of on a Tuesday night. If live music is your thing, Gabah delivers it with more integrity than many places in town.

THE GARAGE

4519 SANTA MONICA BLVD. (AT VIRGIL), SILVERLAKE (323) 662-6802. OPEN MON.–SAT., 9 P.M.–2 A.M., SUN., 5 P.M.–2 A.M. FULL BAR. 21 AND OVER. COVER, FREE–$5. NO FOOD. $$.

Years ago, I was scared to go to the Garage. All the goings-on sounded so hip (Vaginal Davis's Club Sucker), so fervently on the tip, I was afraid I'd wind up crouched in a dark corner with my thumb in my mouth. When I finally got down there, I was sorry I hadn't gone sooner: the former garage space is supercasual, with hubcaps and hoedown doodads on the walls, and the music is often great—loud rockabilly and punk and the theatrics of groups like Los Super Elegantes. The crowd is local, meaning they sport thrift store duds and a zillion tattoos; when they're not drinking lots of beer or hooting at the bands, they're playing pool or checking out what's going on in the back room, where, depending on the night/season/year, you might see a reenactment of the shower scene from *Psycho* or a chick doing a reverse striptease. Because the Garage is always booking new nights, you can make it your regular hangout without seeing the same scene twice.

GARDEN OF EDEN

7080 HOLLYWOOD BLVD. (AT LA BREA), HOLLYWOOD (323) 465-3336. OPEN WED. AND THURS., 10 P.M.–2 A.M.; FRI.–SUN., 9 P.M.–2 A.M.; CLOSED MON. AND TUES. FULL BAR. 21 AND OVER. COVER VARIES. FOOD (CAL-ECLECTIC). $$$.

A former editor of mine, whose knowledge of nightlife could fit in a walnut shell, once suggested I check out the Garden of Eden; this, despite my assuring him it was a horrid "be-seen" sort of place. When he insisted, I told him it was his nickel, and, after one horrendous-bordering-on-hilarious evening, I faxed him an article called "The

Garden of Eden Proves There Is No God." And yet, four years later, The Garden of Eden is still in business! Never underestimate the number of people willing to wait behind a velvet rope; pay a stiff cover to enter an expensively and badly decorated room (think: fake mosque, or Prince in his velvet-and-pendant phase); and then, *because it's there*, stand behind another velvet rope that leads to the VIP balcony. Let me save you the trouble: on the balcony you will find a little Eurotrash, a smattering of men worshipping their own biceps, and the kind of airbrushed faces you see on billboards along the Sunset Strip, all looking down on the people below. Dancing, food, whatever. If you have any taste/self-esteem, avoid the place.

GHENGIS COHEN

740 N. FAIRFAX AVE. (AT MELROSE), WEST HOLLYWOOD (323) 653-0640. OPEN MON.–THURS., NOON–11:30 P.M.; FRI. AND SAT., NOON–12:30 A.M.; SUN., NOON–10:30 P.M. FULL BAR. ALL AGES. COVER VARIES. FOOD (SZECHWAN). $$.

Now here's a wild card: a Chinese restaurant with a Jewish name that's gained a legitimate reputation as one of LA's hottest A and R (that's artists and repertory, to you) hangouts. While the smoked-glass appointments are strictly seventies, the entertainment, mostly acoustic singer-songwriters gunning for a contract, is contemporary (if occasionally too folksy for my taste). Because the Szechwan food is good, I think the way to work Ghengis Cohen is to show up at 8 P.M. (when the music begins), order dinner, and eat while watching the performers triumph or flame out.

THE GIG HOLLYWOOD

7302 MELROSE AVE. (BETWEEN LA BREA AND FAIRFAX, AT POINSETTIA), HOLLYWOOD (323) 936-4440; WWW.LIVEATTHE

GIG.COM. OPEN DAILY, NOON–2 A.M. FULL BAR. 21 AND OVER. COVER, $5–$10. NO FOOD. $$.

The Gig Hollywood is the offspring of the Westside club of the same name. It features live bands (rock, pop, punk, funk, soul) and various nights of the week dedicated to songwriters, unsigned talent, goth, U-name-it. The scene is diffuse: folks of no particular stripe wandering rooms full of overstuffed couches and candelabras—the sort of cheesy pomp I frankly find incongruous with live music, and yet the Gig has proved popular enough to spawn, so what the hell do I know? If you're into live music and live in the area, you might check it out.

THE GIG WEST LA

11637 W. PICO BLVD. (AT BARRINGTON), WEST LA (310) 444-9870; WWW.LIVEATTHEGIG.COM. OPEN DAILY, NOON–2 A.M. FULL BAR. 21 AND OVER. COVER, $5–$10. FOOD (HAMBURGERS AND SUCH). $$.

See above.

GOLDFINGERS

6423 YUCCA ST. (AT CAHUENGA), HOLLYWOOD (323) 962-2913. OPEN DAILY 9 P.M.–2 A.M. FULL BAR. 21 AND OVER. COVER, $3–$5. NO FOOD. $$.

Okay, girls, get out your best Pussy Galore ensembles and head over to this drop-dead-gorgeous cocktail lounge, with tufted gold lamé walls, giant chandeliers, and a sapphire blue fish tank burbling behind the bar. New- and old-school music, from British Invasion to glam, speed-metal to rock, and a debauchery meter that's usually set pretty high. The past several years have seen Goldfingers become even more go-go, with road-tested promoters (e.g.,

Ricky Vodka, Tequila Mockingbird) and celeb deejays (e.g., Taime Down, Coyote Shivers) pulling in the crowds and mixing it up so hard and good, I can hear the howls and growls from here. Little lambs who don't want to be eaten alive (... but in the best way, really) should stay home; all others will have a blast.

GOOD LUCK

1514 HILLHURST AVE. (AT SUNSET), LOS FELIZ (323) 666-3524. OPEN SUN.–THURS., 6 P.M.–MIDNIGHT; FRI. AND SAT., 6 P.M.–2 A.M. FULL BAR. 21 AND OVER. NO COVER. NO FOOD. $$.

Gong! The red-and-gold motif of this mock-mandarin lounge spins the senses as you walk in. . . . You mount a high bamboo stool, and for some mysterious reason order a Singapore Sling, and, drinking in the room and its good-looking habitués, start to think about traveling, yes, traveling—to Molokai? . . . No, further, to Jakarta, where you will ("One more please . . .") write that novel/become a foreign correspondent/fall into a passionate affair with a . . . a pearl smuggler ("Bartender . . ."), to whom you will make love all night in a barely furnished apartment overlooking the Java Sea. This adventure, and more, you will later relate while splayed in the opium den of a room off the bar, occupied by those similarly young and/or bombed enough to dream. Warning: get to Good Luck early on the weekends, or you and a hundred other would-be time travelers will be going nowhere but the line outside.

GRAND AVENUE

1024 S. GRAND AVE. (AT OLYMPIC), DOWNTOWN LA (213) 747-0999. WWW.GRANDNC.COM. OPEN FRI., 8 P.M.–2 A.M.; SAT., 8 P.M.–3 A.M. FULL BAR. 21 AND OVER. COVER, $12–$15; LADIES ENTERING BEFORE 9:30 P.M. GET DISCOUNT. NO FOOD. $$.

This huge Latin club with an arena-size dance floor attracts up to 2,500 people to its weekend clubs. Friday deejays spin salsa and merengue (if you don't know the steps, get out of the way, as many of the dancers are here to move); Saturday there are live salsa bands, with dance lessons available. The crowd, mostly Latino, tends to dress up.

GRAND STAR

943 SUN MUN WAY (AT LEI MIN WAY), CHINATOWN (213) 626-2285. OPEN NIGHTLY, 5 P.M.–1 A.M. FULL BAR. 21 AND OVER IN THE BAR. NO COVER. FOOD (CHINESE). $$.

I suppose people do eat at this large, wonderfully dark Chinese restaurant, though we never seem to make it past the front bar, where, on the weekends, there's always a wacky assortment of drinkers, mostly folks over age 50, listening to the slow-but-steady combo playing standards and a little improvisational jazz. Weeknights, the crowd is a mix of Eastside hipsters and neighborhood Chinese, all of whom sing karaoke, accompanied by those amateur videos showing people tossing bread onto duck ponds or tearfully boarding trains, but never anything to do with the song itself, while the lyrics scroll by in both English and Mandarin. My favorite karaoke spot.

HAL'S

1349 ABBOT KINNEY BLVD. (BETWEEN MAIN AND VENICE), VENICE (310) 396-3105. OPEN SUN.–FRI., 11:30 A.M.–2 A.M.; SAT., 10 A.M.–2 A.M. FULL BAR. ALL AGES. NO COVER. FOOD (CALIFORNIA). $$.

A sleek, modern neighborhood restaurant that's part art gallery/part watering hole, noted for its California cuisine and a bar scene teeming with professionals over age 30. Many people mention how "New York" the place feels (something about SoHo in the early eighties); others posit that it's full of hungry-eyed people looking for a pickup. (Gee, a bar where grown-ups go to meet potential sexual partners. Who knew?) In either case, you can enjoy a good meal at Hal's, as well as the company of locals who appreciate having a high-end hang in the neighborhood and, on Sunday and Monday, a live jazz combo, starting at 9 P.M.

HANK'S

HOTEL STILLWELL, 840 S. GRAND ST. (AT 9TH), DOWNTOWN LA (213) 623-7718. OPEN DAILY, 11 A.M.–2 A.M. FULL BAR. 21 AND OVER. NO COVER. NO FOOD. $.

"More than Just an Outstanding Bar. Also a Way of Life!" So reads the business card of Hank's, where the motto over the bar ("Yesterday's Charm") might easily be applied to the customers, most over age 70 (many are residents upstairs, in the Stillwell Hotel), who pass the afternoon at Hank's slow-drinking, eating free popcorn, and staring at several TVs tuned to AMC. Small and slightly tatty, touched up with 1890s memorabilia, Hank's is a frequent hang for many *LA Times* reporters, as well as drivers ducking out of the storm and stress of Downtown traffic.

HARVELLE'S

1432 4TH ST. (BETWEEN BROADWAY AND SANTA MONICA), SANTA MONICA (310) 395-1676. OPEN NIGHTLY, 8 P.M.–2 A.M. FULL BAR; TWO-DRINK MINIMUM. 21 AND OVER. COVER VARIES. NO FOOD. $$.

This dark and narrow blues club, hosting live music since 1931 (check out the glorious original neon sign), is three-quarters bar, one-quarter performance stage/dance floor, which means you get nose to nose with the sax player and body to body with a crowd of seasoned blues aficionados. While a friend of mine says the lineups have gotten a little "lazy," Harvelle's location—within walking distance from the 3rd Street Promenade—insures a steady stream of locals and tourists alike. Good for business, bad for you: big names bring long lines, so get there early if you want to make it inside.

THE H.M.S. BOUNTY

Gaylord Hotel, 3357 Wilshire Blvd. (between Western and Vermont, at Catalina), LA (213) 385-7275. Open daily, 11 a.m.–2 a.m. Full bar. 21 and over in the bar. No cover. Food (American). $.

Situated off the lobby of the Gaylord Hotel, the Bounty is an LA anachronism: a comfortable, affordable Everyman's bar. With a nautical theme that doesn't appear to have been updated since D-Day—and with a few gentlemen of the right age to have participated in that invasion bellied up to the bar, as often as not reading the racing forms—the Bounty is passing its charm on to the next generation: 20-somethings piled into high-back booths, glugging cocktails and recollecting how, when they were kids, their parents used to take them to places *just like this*. As with any bar of this ilk, you can also dine, on such bygone classics as filet of sole *almondine* and beef stroganoff. But be warned: I have known several young bachelors who became such fixtures at the Bounty, they took rooms upstairs, and became quickly enamored of the fact that everything they needed—laundry service, food, booze—could be had without leaving the premises. A concept that, depending on your point of view, is utopian or prematurely tragic.

HOLLYWOOD BILLIARDS

5750 Hollywood Blvd. (between Gower and Western, at Wilton), Hollywood (323) 465-0115. www.hollywoodbilliardsla.com. Open daily, 11 a.m.–2:30 a.m. Full bar. All ages. No cover. Food (Northern Italian). $$.

The old Hollywood Billiards, on the corner of Western and Hollywood, caved in on itself after the Northridge earthquake, which was no surprise to anyone who'd been to that bare-bones pool hall. The new Hollywood Billiards is bigger and cleaner, and you don't need to walk down that rickety flight of steps. It's also closer to the heart of Hollywood and open really late, and, since it has 40 tables, it's usually pretty easy to shoot a game.

HOLLYWOOD STAR LANES

5227 Santa Monica Blvd. (three blocks east of Western), Hollywood (323) 665-4111. Open daily, 24 hours. All ages. Full bar. No cover. Food (snack bar). $.

The attractions here include beautiful neon (which you can see to good advantage in *The Big Lebowski*) and a snug, dark cocktail lounge. In addition, the place is open round the clock. Everyone bowls at Hollywood Star Lanes: hipsters and insomniacs, retirees and teenagers, families fooling around and pros practicing strikes. Which means that, at peak times, it can get busy. At four in the morning, however, you usually have the lanes to yourself.

HOP LOUIE

950 Mei Ling Way (west of N. Broadway), Chinatown (213) 628-4244. Open daily, 1 p.m.–2 a.m. Full bar. 21 and over. No cover. Food upstairs (Chinese). $.

Each time I walk into this teeny bar beneath a Chinese restaurant, I feel as though I'm in a movie. A typical night: You part the curtain in the doorway and see that, besides yourself and the bartender wiping a glass (always wiping a glass), the only inhabitants are a table full of ancient Asian men playing mah-jongg. You order a drink. You watch part of a ball game playing silently on the TV behind that inscrutable bartender. A few film-production types arrive, speaking amongst themselves in low tones. Then, in a recessed corner, you notice a large man in a fedora—was he always here, or have you just noticed him? He lifts his face. My god, he looks exactly like Orson Welles. Is he smiling at you? Was that a signal? Where did the Chinese men go? And why is the bartender laughing? Ten miles from Hollywood, within sight of Downtown's skyscrapers, and yet everything appears foreign, decipherable only in cinematic terms. Perhaps you will not experience Hop Louie this way, but I do, every time.

HOUSE OF BLUES

8430 SUNSET BLVD. (BETWEEN CRESCENT HEIGHTS AND LA CIENEGA), WEST HOLLYWOOD (323) 848-5100. OPEN NIGHTLY, SHOW TIMES VARY. FULL BAR. 21 AND OVER. COVER, $10–$25. FOOD (AMERICAN AND CAJUN). $$$.

I'm gonna eat it on this one, because what I really want is to not include the House of Blues at all, for the following reasons: the plethora of corporate crap for sale; the neck-monster security goons who'd as soon toss you as tell you where the bathroom is; and the atrocious parking, an insult I would not wish on anyone—$10 so you can wait 45 minutes for your car, during which time you get to listen to some idiot yell at his limo driver. Never, never again! But then I remember that I saw Johnny Cash there, and if he plays the House of Blues, there must be something right about the place—nearly that it's big enough to draw big names, but small enough so you can see the show and even get up close. But that's as far as I'm going.

JAX BAR AND GRILL

339 N. BRAND. (AT CALIFORNIA), GLENDALE (818) 500-1604. OPEN DAILY, 11 A.M.–2 A.M. FULL BAR. ALL AGES. NO COVER. FOOD (STEAKS, SEAFOOD, PASTA). $$.

A lunch spot and supper club, with a daily Happy Hour accompanied by piano music and, every night at 9 P.M., solid, straight-ahead jazz, punctuated by the occasional blues band. While the layout—a long, narrow room, with lots of whimsical stained glass—looks more ice-cream parlor than jazz club, the patrons give off a pleasant "we live in Glendale" vibe, the music is the real thing, and the weekend scene heats up nicely. A prime local spot, and a nice place to stop after a day at the Galleria.

JAZZ BAKERY

3233 HELMS AVE. (SOUTH OF VENICE BLVD.), CULVER CITY (310) 271-9039. WWW.THEJAZZBAKERY.COM. OPEN NIGHTLY, TIMES VARY DEPENDING ON SHOW. BEER AND WINE ONLY. ALL AGES. COVER, $12–$22. SNACKS. $$.

The place to go for straight jazz, no chaser, from heavyweight international talent to local stars. A hangar-size room with no tables, no drink service (you can grab something from the café in the lobby), and nothing to interfere with the music, the Jazz Bakery is often the only LA stop for some of jazz's big names. Bring folks who appreciate the real thing.

JAZZ SPOT (LOS FELIZ RESTAURANT)

2138 HILLHURST AVE. (ONE BLOCK SOUTH OF LOS FELIZ), LOS FELIZ (323) 666-8666. HTTP://LOSFELIZJAZZSPOT.COM. OPEN

TUES.–SAT., 8:00 P.M.–2 A.M.; CLOSED MON., JAZZ SPOT DARK ON SUN. FULL BAR. ALL AGES. COVER VARIES. FOOD (CALIFORNIA-FRENCH, IN ADJACENT RESTAURANT). $$.

When I walked into this jazz club for the first time, I thought, how pretty! The creamy, urbane room is fitted out with the booths and glass panels from the original Chasen's, and the feel is ultraluxe. So, apparently, is the food: the critics have fallen all over themselves to praise chef Collin Crannell's cuisine. Yet the restaurant's only half the story: behind the dining area is a seriously good-looking and expansive performance space, with great acoustics, a nine-foot Yamaha grand piano, and a big bandstand where you can expect to find excellent jazz and fiery vocalists. Exactly the type of serious yet mellow night spot that Los Feliz, awash in lounges and local bars, can use.

JEWEL'S CATCH ONE

4067 PICO BLVD. (TWO BLOCKS EAST OF CRENSHAW), LA (323) 734-8849. OPEN MON., WED., AND THURS., 5 P.M.–2 A.M.; FRI. AND SAT., 5 P.M.–4 A.M., SOMETIMES LATER; CLOSED TUES. FULL BAR. 21 AND OVER. COVER VARIES. NO FOOD, EXCEPT SPECIAL OCCASIONS (SEE BELOW). $$.

You want a mostly lesbian-and-gay, all-color, extravagant club and disco where you can play pool? I know just the place. Different shows nightly, from exotica to go-go dancers, female impersonators to karaoke, old-school jazz and blues to Lakers nights (the latter featuring a buffet in front of a big-screen TV). And every night there's dancing, in a humongous room with the sweet "let's get down!" quality of a high school auditorium decked out for the 1979 prom, where things there always get sweaty and funky and fun.

THE JOINT

8771 W. PICO BLVD. (AT ROBERTSON), WEST LA (310) 275-2619. OPEN NIGHTLY, 8 P.M.–2 A.M. FULL BAR. 21 AND OVER. COVER VARIES. FOOD (PIZZA). $$.

Four bands a night, seven nights a week, in a long room with a bizarre, bachelor-gone-berserk motif: plush black carpet, gilt mirrors, elephant tusks mounted over the stage. O-Kay. Yet somehow the Joint pulls it off, mostly because the music—hip-hop, alternative, and country-rock—is consistently good, but also because the crowd is young and forgiving, happy to be able to get a drink in under ten minutes (the bar is long, and the bartenders are fast) and to have a little room in which to dance and a little something to eat. Good midway-between-East-and-Westside location.

THE JOKER

2827 PICO BLVD. (AT 29TH ST.), WEST LA (310) 828-9235. OPEN DAILY, 6 A.M.–2 A.M. FULL BAR. 21 AND OVER. NO COVER. NO FOOD. $.

Years ago, an editor asked if I could *please* cover more bars on the Westside, and so, one rainy night, I found myself trawling for cocktails on a no-man's stretch of Pico, about to gas it until I saw a sign shaped like a playing card over an open doorway. It was a bar, yes, but not one I could write about for the glossies: a box of a room with no character, cheap liquor, and a sparse, heavy-drinking clientele. I sat next to an American Indian partway through a sex change, who was waiting or not waiting for money to finish the operation, and who stopped midway through her narrative, clearly bone-tired and bored talking about it. I have only been back to the Joker a handful of times, partly because one doesn't drive 15 miles from home to drink in a dive, but also because, as with any bar full of people who've resigned themselves to sticking to the stool, it hurts to drink there. Which is also why I recommend it.

JONES

7205 SANTA MONICA BLVD. (TWO BLOCKS WEST OF LA BREA, AT FORMOSA), WEST HOLLYWOOD (323) 850-1727. OPEN NIGHTLY, 7 P.M.–1:30 A.M.; ALSO OPEN FOR LUNCH, MON.–FRI., NOON–4:30 P.M., AND FOR COCKTAILS 4:30 P.M.–7 P.M. FULL BAR. 21 AND OVER. NO COVER. FOOD (ECLECTIC). $$.

Every time I walk into this savagely hip, throbbing-with-color room, I feel as though the theme music from some early-1970s detective show should start playing, and some guy in a mustache—maybe Burt Reynolds as Dan August—should sidle up, Jack Daniel's in hand, and stare down my cleavage. I don't think I'm the only one who feels this way, as the temperature in this swell-looking bar and restaurant always makes one feel, shall we say, poised for action. While Jones also serves really good food—outstanding thin-crust pizza, an artichoke with two aiolis, deep-dish apple pie with caramel sauce—most people are content to merely feast their eyes on the luscious habitués. Go when you feel like being devoured.

J. SLOAN'S

8623 MELROSE AVE. (TWO BLOCKS EAST OF SAN VINCENTE), WEST HOLLYWOOD (310) 659-0250. OPEN DAILY, 11 A.M.–2 A.M. FULL BAR. 21 AND OVER. NO COVER. FOOD (BURGERS, ETC.). $$.

This corner pub qualifies as one of the oldest in the city: open continuously since 1919. Friendly and unpretentious, drawing a huge crowd of sports fans whenever the local teams play, and throngs of party regulars every evening, it's also a welcoming place to grab a burger (on home-baked bread) and a beer in the afternoon.

JUMBO'S CLOWN ROOM

5153 HOLLYWOOD BLVD. (BETWEEN WESTERN AND NORMANDIE, AT WINONA), HOLLYWOOD (323) 666-1187. WWW.JUMBOS.COM. OPEN DAILY, 2 P.M.–2 A.M. FULL BAR. 21 AND OVER. NO COVER. NO FOOD. $.

My friend Sharon recently told me that she'd found a counter on her computer that keeps track of how many games of solitaire she's played: 10,801. I sometimes fear that, somewhere in the universe, there's a tally of how many hours I've spent in Jumbo's, a small strip bar started, so I'm told, by a former carny. I keep coming for a lot of reasons: There's never a cover, which makes it the perfect place to meet people with whom to start an evening; the dancers are a varied lot (burlesque and baby-doll, strung-out lasses and modern dance students, marvels on the pole and those who "smoke" cigarettes in unexpected orifices); and, because they don't make a lot in tips, most of these dancers can't afford implants, which I find refreshing. And talk about manners: after her two-song set, each girl, dressed in something nominally more concealing, comes onto the floor and shakes the hand of every customer. While there are certainly strip places with more polish, I'll take the hospitality of Jumbo's any day.

KANE

5574 MELROSE AVE. (AT GOWER), HOLLYWOOD (323) 466-6263. OPEN MON.–FRI., 6 P.M.–2 A.M., SAT. AND SUN., 8 P.M.–2 A.M. FULL BAR. 21 AND OVER. COVER VARIES, FREE–$10. NO FOOD. $$.

I can't decide what Kane resembles: Space Age bachelor pad? High-concept airport lounge? Someplace where both Ray Eames and Superfly would hang out? Whatever it is, I like it. I like the big, square, coral-colored leather stools; I like the brain-popping funk they spin on weekends (and the bikini-clad, hyperkinetic go-go dancers gyrating on-stage); and I very much like the owner, Ivan Kane, whose New York brand of magnanimity makes everyone glad they came. If you work at Paramount, or know someone who does, this is the perfect spot (two blocks away) to meet for an after-work drink.

KEY CLUB

9039 SUNSET BLVD. (ONE BLOCK EAST OF DOHENY), WEST HOLLYWOOD (310) 274-5800. WWW.THEKEYCLUB.NET. OPEN NIGHTLY, 8 P.M.–2 A.M. FULL BAR. 21 AND OVER. COVER VARIES. FOOD (CALIFORNIA). $$.

Doing their part to encourage the burgeoning *Blade Runner* ambiance of the Sunset Strip, the Key Club has installed a massive video feed on the front of the building so you don't miss the point that, inside, rock stars are doing things like (... cue the Roger Daltry scream prelude to "We Won't Be Fooled Again") swinging their hair and smashing their guitars and making the girlies weak in the knees. Big multiroomed club with lots of purple laser lighting, an elevated yet intimate stage that lets performers radiate "I am rock god—worship me!" by merely standing there, and lots and lots of music, from Rob Zombie to James Brown, Fishbone to Tongue. Rock rules!

KING EDWARD SALOON

131 E. 5TH ST. (AT LOS ANGELES), DOWNTOWN LA (213) 629-2023. OPEN DAILY, 6 A.M.–2 A.M. (SOMETIMES EARLIER). FULL BAR. 21 AND OVER. NO COVER. FOOD (SANDWICHES). $.

A bar lover's bar, serving SRO residents and assorted locals, almost all of whom are 65 if they're a day, and almost all of whom are happy to stand young people a round. Very friendly, very cheap, King Eddy's is the sort of place where you stop for one beer and wind up staying three hours, shooting the shit with folks who keep stopping at the table, asking about your life and telling you about theirs. Not much in the way of looks but perfect as it is, with a big oval bar, a few tables along one wall, and lots of Downtown color.

THE KNITTING FACTORY HOLLYWOOD

7021 HOLLYWOOD BLVD. (ONE BLOCK EAST OF LA BREA), HOLLYWOOD (323) 463-0204. WWW.KNITTINGFACTORY.COM. OPEN NIGHTLY, 11 A.M.–2 A.M. FULL BAR. ALL AGES. COVER VARIES. FOOD ("ECLECTIC FUSION"). $$$.

Long-known in New York for giving stage to a broad spectrum of musicians and performing artists, the Knitting Factory recently opened an LA branch, promising to bring its "downtown philosophy" to the Walk of Fame. This philosophy apparently translates into a club that feels like a shopping mall (and is in fact part of one, since the Knitting Factory is situated in the west corner of the GCC Hollywood Galaxy)—an impersonal cube of chrome and glass and computer screens (for live feed from the New York club); an imposing ticket booth off the not-so-cozy bar; the narrow Alterknit Lounge for smaller acts (a room that feels so Beat Generation, I expected the audience to snap their fingers in appreciation); and the larger Main Stage, which, in its first month alone, was host to such diverse performers as Wiskey Bisquit, Snoop Doggy Dogg, and Odetta. Despite its somewhat sterile feel, I am sure every local highbrow will swear the Knitting Factory is exactly the sort of venue LA needs; this, right before they head home to watch *Spectacular Freeway Chases III*.

THE LAB

835 S. SPRING ST. (AT 8TH), DOWNTOWN LA (213) 689-4725. WWW.CHANNEL-X.COM/LAB/ART.HTML. HOURS AND DAYS VARY. NO ALCOHOL. ALL AGES SOME NIGHTS/21 AND OVER OTHER NIGHTS. COVER, FREE–$10. NO FOOD. $.

The Lab owner and curator Amber Pierson has turned a gigantic downtown loft into one of LA's most trenchant galleries and performance spaces. What will you experience there? Everything from outsider art to boudoir shows, punk rock to ambient pop, raves to Sunday brunch. Pierson has dubbed her space an "epistemological gallery system," and if you hang around the Lab with any regularity, you will indeed have every one of your corporeal senses engaged. The Downtown crowd is young, arty and cottoning to just about anything, so long as it's vital, something Pierson has the nose and eye for. Very cool spot. Don't worry about your car, there's secure parking in the lot next door.

LA FONDA DE LOS CAMPEROS

2501 WILSHIRE BLVD. (TWO BLOCKS WEST OF ALVARADO), LOS ANGELES (213) 380-5055. OPEN SUN.–THURS., 5:30 P.M.–MIDNIGHT, FRI. AND SAT., 5:30 P.M.–1:30 A.M.; CLOSED MON. FULL BAR. ALL AGES. NO COVER. FOOD (MEXICAN). $$.

An enormous, dramatic Mexican restaurant with a drinking area so dark, one literally needs to feel one's way into the bar until the eyes adjust. Tasty, sweet margaritas, a good (if not extensive) menu, and mariachi music every night. Ah, but not the mariachi you may be used to, where four fat guys hover around the table strumming for tips. Los

Camperos are a dozen men in gorgeous regalia, playing on an elevated, charmingly painted stage. Their singing travels between delicate and vigorous, jubilant and heartbreaking. Every third song, a pair of dancers appears, in never-less-than-dazzling costume, stamping boots and swirling skirts for the (mostly Mexican) families that come here, often to celebrate a birthday. Bring the kids, who will be over the moon at the entertainment. La Fonda is also a revivifying spot to spend Happy Hour.

LA POUBELLE

5907 FRANKLIN AVE. (AT BRONSON), HOLLYWOOD (323) 465-0807. OPEN NIGHTLY, 5:30 P.M.–1:30 A.M. FULL BAR. ALL AGES. NO COVER. FOOD (FRENCH). $$.

One's take on La Poubelle depends, I suppose, on one's perspective. To some, it's a replica of Parisian café culture, with arty types engaging in fevered tête-à-têtes, drinking bottle after bottle of wine, falling in love and into arguments. Turn the prism, and these same people appear arrogant and merely loud. The last time my sweetheart and I were there, when the officious owner stared at the slimy *poulet* we'd waited an hour for and declared that, "Zis is 'ow we make it 'ere," and the drunk French boy at the table next to us knocked over his drink for the fourth time while trying to sketch me on a napkin, I thought my slow-to-boil boyfriend would throw his chair through the window and onto the diners at the outdoor tables on Franklin. One man's charm is another's raw chicken.

LARGO

432 N. FAIRFAX AVE. (BETWEEN MELROSE AND BEVERLY), LA (323) 852-1073. OPEN MON.–SAT., 8 P.M.–2 A.M.; CLOSED SUN. FULL BAR. ALL AGES. COVER, $2–$12. FOOD (BISTRO). $$.

A thinking man's cabaret, with an everything-as-long-as-it's-interesting and/or has-a-sense-of-humor booking policy that includes sharp songwriters (Aimee Mann, Michael Penn, Grant Lee Phillips, Neil Finn), comedy, "Hawaiian slack guitar," torch singers, spoken word, and more in a simple, sort of raw supper club setting, with a little bar in the back for those who want to sip and mingle. An interesting and fun place, and a must if you like a little provocation with your entertainment.

LAS PALMAS SUPPER CLUB

1714 N. LAS PALMAS AVE. (AT HOLLYWOOD BLVD.), HOLLYWOOD (323) 464-0171. OPEN MON.–THURS., 8 P.M.–2 A.M.; FRI. AND SAT., 7 P.M.–2 A.M. FULL BAR. 21 AND OVER. COVER VARIES. FOOD (MEXICAN/ASIAN). $$$.

There used to be a punk club and a little Mexican restaurant on the corner of Las Palmas and Hollywood. While I wasn't there for the actual demolition of these places, I imagine it went something like this: the scythe known as "Bigger! Better! Now!" swings, slaying the small and the quaint so that Another Velvet Rope Emporium may live. Then, the PR people sound the clarion call, and of-the-minute scenesters flock from thither and yon, to this large, expensive club, with two well-appointed smoking patios, supper club dining, and a revolving roster of scenes, depending on which promoter books the night. (Currently: Brent Bolthouse on Wednesdays; Jeff Goldblum on piano with the Mildred Snitzer Orchestra on Mondays.) Do guests need to have their name on any number of VIP lists to gain admittance? Of course! Will they often show up at Las Palmas and find there's a private party with attendant klieg lights underway? Yes!

Will Las Palmas have been supplanted by the Next Velvet Rope Emporium by the time you read this? Live by the sword...

LAVA LOUNGE

1533 N. LA BREA AVE. (A HALF BLOCK NORTH OF SUNSET), HOLLYWOOD (323) 876-6612. OPEN DAILY, 9 P.M.–2 A.M. FULL BAR. 21 AND OVER. COVER, $3–$5. NO FOOD. $$.

A hipster lounge/Tiki bar in the heart of Hollywood, Lava Lounge is a beautiful thing, with a palm-thatched ceiling, sissy-back barstools, abalone-inlaid tables, and a big gurgling fish tank backing the tropical bar. While the room is fantastical (think: Tim Burton does Don Ho), the music is serious: jazz, funk, disco, and the occasional appearance of LA's best surf band, the Blue Hawaiians. With the tiny, torrid dance floor inducing ardor, the oversize *mai-tai*s spilling fruit, and the twinkle lights turning from sapphire to gold to electric rose and back again, it's easy to become entranced at Lava. And if you swoon, don't worry: Chris (also known as the nicest door guy in town) will be there to catch you.

LE COLONIAL

8783 BEVERLY BLVD. (A HALF BLOCK EAST OF ROBERTSON), LA (310) 289-0660. RESTAURANT OPEN MON.–FRI., NOON–3 P.M.; SUN.–THURS., 6 P.M.–10 P.M., FRI. AND SAT., UNTIL 11 P.M.; BAR OPEN NIGHTLY, 6 P.M.–2 A.M. ALL AGES IN THE RESTAURANT, 21 AND OVER IN THE BAR. OCCASIONAL COVER. FOOD (VIETNAMESE-FRENCH). $$$.

A thumbnail history of Le Colonial: an exotic, expensive Vietnamese-French restaurant and bar has a meteoric rise, becomes a renowned pickup spot, lies low for a while.

Then, like the phoenix from its ashes, it rises, having worked a little intellectualism and entertainment into its beauty-for-beauty's-sake regime, and voilà, everyone flocks back, especially for the monthly **Spoken Interludes,** a literary salon combining a buffet and readings. (For details: info@spokeninterlude.com; for reservations: (323) 957-4688.) As always, the two-level Le Colonial is extremely pretty, and the downstairs restaurant is an idealized version of Saigon, 1960—an expanse of rattan, green tiles, palm fronds, and ceiling fans. The upstairs bar is lush and evocative, the lighting lower, the mood sexier; several nights a week, deejays spin ambient, trip-hop, and jazz for the still lithe and lovely, mostly Westside crowd.

LES DEUX CAFÉ

1638 N. Las Palmas Ave. (a half block south of Hollywood), Hollywood (323) 465-0509. Open for lunch Mon.–Fri., noon–2 p.m.; for dinner, Mon.–Sat., 6:30 p.m.–11 p.m.; bar/cabaret open until 2 a.m.; closed Sun. Full bar. All ages in the restaurant; 21 and over in bar/cabaret. No cover. Food (French). $$$.

A glittering soirée that is part Provençal café, part performance art. Every night an effulgent wave of the pretty and the powerful rolls through the beautiful, flower-festooned garden, the warm and woody dining areas, and the beautiful bar/cabaret, which looks like a British men's club but is as likely to feature drag queens as piano music. The food can be magnificent, and the mood, while constantly threatening to pitch into too-fabulous land, manages to perch right where it needs to: generous enough to lure the ravishing habitués, egoistic enough to feed the diva that is the club itself. A must in Hollywood.

LIQUID KITTY

11780 W. PICO BLVD. (BETWEEN BARRINGTON AND BUNDY), WEST LA (310) 473-3707. WWW.THEKITTY.COM. OPEN MON.–FRI., 6 P.M.–2 A.M., SAT. AND SUN., 8 P.M.–2 A.M. FULL BAR. 21 AND OVER. NO COVER. NO FOOD. $$.

One of the Westside's few worthy cocktail lounges, Liquid Kitty is a cool drink of water for locals tired of schlepping to Hollywood to get a goddamn drink. Clubby and dark, Liquid Kitty's best early on, when you can hear yourself over the sound system and get a seat before everyone else west of La Cienega with a taste for the lounge life beats you to it. Better yet, snag one of the cozy back booths.

LITTLE JOY

1477 SUNSET BLVD. (BETWEEN ALVARADO AND ELYSIAN PARK, AT PORTIA), ECHO PARK (213) 250-3417. OPEN 4 P.M.–2 A.M. FULL BAR. 21 AND OVER. NO COVER. NO FOOD. $.

"Looks like a place men go to escape their wives. Oh, wait," said my friend Jenny, seeing her error. My impression that the Little Joy—a hybrid old-guy gay bar/Mexican pool joint—lives up to its name may be attributable to the less-than-balmy reception given the fair sex. Nevertheless, the room is bare-bones cute—a boxy oblong with two small pool tables, tinsely *quinces* decorations, pool tournament trophies, and one poster of Tom Berringer—making it a good, anonymous locale in which to leave the world behind.

LOLA'S

945 N. FAIRFAX AVE. (TWO BLOCKS NORTH OF MELROSE), WEST HOLLYWOOD (213) 736-5652. OPEN NIGHTLY, 5:30 P.M.–1:30 A.M. FULL BAR. 21 AND OVER IN BAR AREA. NO COVER. FOOD (CALIFORNIA). $$.

The perennially popular hangout of the fit and the fabulous and those who aspire to be. Two large, airy, shabby-chic rooms that feel more Westhampton than West Hollywood, inhabited by gorgeous actor/model types sipping apple martinis and gossiping about pilot season and Pilates. Reportedly fine Cal-cuisine (which I cannot comment on, having stuck to the deservedly lauded martinis) and an overall tenor that typifies a certain element of Los Angeles: in short, those who take pains to be attractive, to make the right connections, and to become part of the entertainment terra firma before the sun has sizzled away their every last gram of collagen.

LOUIS XIV

606 N. LA BREA AVE. (ONE BLOCK SOUTH OF MELROSE), HOLLYWOOD (323) 934-5102. WWW.LOUISXIV.NET. OPEN NIGHTLY, 6 P.M.–2 A.M. FULL BAR. OVER 21. NO COVER WITH DINNER RESERVATIONS OR BEFORE 10 P.M.; COVER VARIES AFTER 10 P.M. FOOD (FRENCH). $$.

By day, Louis XIV is almost certainly the closest LA comes to a French café: intimate and Provençal inside, with lots of nooks and crannies in which to snuggle and hide, and outdoor tables full of real and faux Europeans grateful to have found a spot at which to linger in notoriously driven LA. After 9 P.M., however, the scene heats up, with French (and other) deejays spinning electronic dance, down-tempo grooves, and hip-hop. Long-running nights, like **Monday's Special,** attract a loyal crowd and the occasional celeb deejay. If you like to dance, Louis XIV offers a pleasant shift from factorylike clubs.

LOWENBRAU KELLER RESTAURANT

3211 BEVERLY BLVD. (EAST OF HOOVER), LA (213) 382-

5723. Open Mon.–Sat., 11:30 a.m.–11 p.m.; closed Sun. Full bar. All ages. No cover. Food (German). $$.

Mein Gott! I passed this German restaurant 500 times and never suspected what was inside: an insanely opulent room, with 10 million wine bottles/flowers/doodads on every scintilla of surface, chandeliers the size of Volkswagens, and a piano festooned with framed portraits in memoriam. "It looks as though Versace swept through a Milwaukee beer hall," gasped my friend Diane as we settled into one of the ludicrously overstuffed booths for a lunch of schnitzel and sauerbraten. (The hulking, six-foot-two German waitress glowered when Diane tried to order fish; she changed her order.) At the front of the restaurant is a small leather wraparound bar where you can enjoy a stein of hefeweizen or a glass of Gewürztraminer. While Lowenbrau is a little out-of-the way and down at the heels, it's worth the trip; be assured the place will knock the eyes out of anyone you take there.

MAMAGAYA

401 N. La Cienega Blvd. (between Melrose and Beverly), LA (310) 659-4999. Open nightly, 7:30 p.m.–2 a.m. Full bar. 21 and over. Cover after 9:30 p.m., $10. Food (eclectic). $$.

A pancultural hothouse of a club with a great big cruisable bar, leopard print seating areas, a dining room that serves everything from pasta to sushi to soul, and live Latin/Jamaican/Cuban music. Oh, and a laser-lit fertility god over the door. I never just stop here for a drink, but go for the whole evening, starting in the bar, working through a little food, and then staying for the music and the company, which is always sharp and sexy. One word of advice: dress up, as everyone else does. Note to Lakers fans: Shaq helped Kobe celebrate his 21st birthday here.

MARTINI LOUNGE

5657 MELROSE AVE. (TWO BLOCKS EAST OF VINE), HOLLYWOOD (323) 467-4068. OPEN NIGHTLY, 9 P.M.–2 A.M. FULL BAR. 21 AND OVER. COVER, $3–$10. FOOD (SUSHI BAR). $$.

A perennially popular lounge/club featuring local rock and pop lineups most nights, with an occasional comedy night. The rooms are sexy, with cozy banquettes and low lighting, and there's a sizable smoking patio. And then there's the dance floor, which, at least to me, can become so hot it feels like a concrete coffin. Nevertheless, a popular Hollywood hang for junior hipsters.

MAX'S BAR AND LOUNGE

442 N. FAIRFAX AVE. (BETWEEN MELROSE AND BEVERLY), LA (323) 651-4421. OPEN MON.–SAT., 6 P.M.–2 A.M.; SUN., 5 P.M.–2 A.M. FULL BAR. 21 AND OVER. NO COVER. FOOD (ECLECTIC NOSHES). $$.

I really like this bar, which my boyfriend describes as "a cross between a coven and a roadhouse." It's very small, fitting perhaps 20 comfortably, with leopard print booths, interesting paintings/photographs on the walls, low lighting, and a shimmering bar. The bartenders are super-friendly and usually adorable, and the crowd always seems kind and smart—down with what's going on but not trying to push any style too hard. The best place to drink in the Fairfax area.

MCCABE'S GUITAR SHOP

3101 PICO BLVD. (AT 31ST ST.), SANTA MONICA (310) 828-4497 (GUITAR SHOP); (310) 828-4403 (CONCERT LINE). SHOWS FRI. AND SAT., THE OCCASIONAL SUN. NO ALCOHOL. ALL AGES. COVER, $10–$20. NO FOOD. $$.

One place that takes itself and its music very seriously is McCabe's, a guitar shop cum performance space that feels more like a place of worship. So grave is the audience that they file through the guitar shop before the weekend shows to admire the instruments as though they were Paleolithic artifacts. Okay, maybe I'm a cynic, or simply born too late to believe that music has the power to change the world. All I know is that every time I've been to McCabe's, it's been a very earnest experience, with everyone hushed and stock-still lest we offend... who? The musicians? They always seem all right. The performance room is almost always hotter than hell, too, and because McCabe's serves no drinks (of course), you just have to sit there and take it. And woe to you if you're seated behind a pole: because moving is prohibited, that's what you'll stare at all night.

MEMORIES

1074 N. Tustin Ave. (100 yards north of 91 Fwy.), Anaheim (714) 630-9232. http://memories.dhs.org. Open nightly, 7:30 p.m.–midnight; Mon. and Thurs. until 1 a.m., Fri. and Sat., until 2 a.m. Full bar. All ages. Cover $5; $8–$10 with dance lesson. Food (Italian). $$.

A little out-of-the-way, but a swear-by for real lindy-hoppers and West Coast swingers who make the trip to dance at this 1940s-style supper club. Superfriendly, with great big rooms and three lightly springy hardwood dance floors, which the management says "move with you" so your feet never tire. Big bands most nights, with the occasional salsa and ballroom night. Don't feel like driving to Anaheim? Check out Memories' Web-cam, which beams live most nights, 9 p.m.–midnight.

MICELI'S

1646 N. LAS PALMAS AVE. (A HALF BLOCK SOUTH OF HOLLYWOOD), HOLLYWOOD (323) 466-3438. OPEN DAILY, 11 A.M.–2 P.M. FULL BAR. ALL AGES. NO COVER. FOOD (ITALIAN). $$.

An informal Italian restaurant (checkered tablecloths, Chianti bottles lining the walls) with a cozy, elevated bar, excellent piano music most nights, and the sort of scene where nothing is required but that you sit, relax, have a glass of wine, and maybe contemplate that painting of the Mona Lisa smiling down on a pizza. A neighborhood favorite since it opened in 1949, it's a very nice place to come early in the evening for a few glasses of wine and a little chat.

MING'S DYNASTY

5221 HOLLYWOOD BLVD. (BETWEEN WESTERN AND NORMANDIE, AT HARVARD), HOLLYWOOD (323) 462-2039. OPEN DAILY, 8 P.M.–2 A.M. FULL BAR. 21 AND OVER. NO COVER. NO FOOD. $.

Ming's is a gay bar frequented by middle-aged Asian and white dudes and the occasional interloper, though there aren't many: I do not exaggerate when I say I passed this place 2,000 times before I realized it was a bar. The area's no beauty—Ming's is adjacent to an SRO hotel on the crumbling east end of Hollywood Boulevard—and the room's just serviceable, a horizontal box with a big oval bar and a few pool tables in the back. Its one splashy bit is a big-screen TV mounted in the corner, which shows a selection of early eighties videos (Boy George, Michael Jackson, Bananarama, Duran Duran, et al.) that today look positively other-planetary.

THE MINT

6010 PICO BLVD. (AT CRESCENT HEIGHTS), LA (323) 954-9630. WWW.THEMINTHOLLYWOOD.COM. OPEN SUN.–THURS.,

7:30 P.M.–12:30 P.M., FRI. AND SAT., 7:30 P.M.–2 A.M. FULL BAR. ALL AGES. COVER, $5–$10. FOOD (CAJUN-ECLECTIC). $$.

This onetime hole-in-the-wall blues joint underwent a metaphysical miracle in the midnineties: it tripled in size, added a gleaming full bar, an expanded Southern menu, and a cocktail-table/cozy-booth floor plan that puts one in mind of a forties supper club. But owner Jed Ojeda, who lives and bleeds blues, would be galled if all I wrote was how swell the place looks. The Mint was, is, and always will be about serious live music: blues and jazz, rhythm and blues and swing, and a little rockabilly, with a layout that lets you get right up close to players like Taj Mahal, Royal Crown Review, and Ben Lee. (Thanks to the great acoustics, the Mint does live recording here as well.) There are hundreds of places to hear music in LA, but only a handful that are serious and wonderful at once. The Mint is one of them.

MOLLY MALONE'S

575 S. FAIRFAX AVE. (ONE BLOCK NORTH OF WILSHIRE), LA (323) 935-1577. OPEN DAILY, 9 A.M.–2 A.M. FULL BAR. 21 AND OVER. COVER AFTER 8:30 P.M. (CHECK TIME), $3–$5. FOOD (SANDWICHES). $$.

Guess what kind of bar? A well-worn and long-loved Irish pub, with Guinness and other British imports on tap, a healthy number of regulars, and live music most nights, often a lineup of Celtic folksingers, though occasionally rhythm and blues or rock. (I've also heard Irish poets read here.) A good local spot, but if you're planning on drinking your green beer here on St. Patrick's Day, get to Molly Malone's early: by noon, the crowd is spilling out the door.

MR. T'S BOWL

5621½ N. FIGUEROA AVE. (AT AVE. 57), HIGHLAND PARK (323) 256-7561 OR (323) 960-5693. BAR OPEN DAILY, 8 A.M.–2 A.M., "IF THE CROWD DESERVES IT"; MUSIC, TUES.–SUN., STARTING AT AROUND 9 P.M. FULL BAR. 21 AND OVER. COVER VARIES. NO FOOD. $.

Need an antidote to Hollywood bullshit? Head over to Highland Park, to this former bowling alley (I'll give you a dollar if you can suss out where the lanes were) that now houses a dive bar and a stage/seating area that looks like a high school auditorium. Add twinkle lights, a fish tank, and a few photos of Ronald Reagan, and you have one of the most authentically game venues in town. Six or so bands (punk, pop, goth, garage) play here most nights, for a crowd that runs from skate-rats to Bohos to local boozers. I love Mr. T's because it feels like being out of LA, in the kind of club small-town freaks create because every other place within 50 miles sucks. Favorite fantasy: dropping a few ICM agents in the middle of Mr. T's and watching them try to figure it out.

MUSSO & FRANK GRILL

6667 HOLLYWOOD BLVD. (BETWEEN HIGHLAND AND CAHUENGA, AT CHEROKEE), HOLLYWOOD (323) 467-7788. OPEN TUES.–SAT., 11 A.M.–11 P.M.; CLOSED SUN. AND MON. FULL BAR. ALL AGES. NO COVER. FOOD (AMERICAN). $$.

Every time I enter Musso & Frank's, I feel slightly giddy, and grateful. Hollywood's oldest restaurant (open since 1919) is big as a ship's ballroom, with 50-foot-high ceilings, tuxedoed career waiters who brook no indecision (not an easy task, with over 150 items on the menu), and a crowd that defies categorization: fat cats cutting deals; club kids wearing Cons; tourists, birthday celebrants, movie stars, and anyone who enjoys a great steak, shoestring fries, and creamed spinach. And then there's the bar, a long thin beauty gleaming with glass and mirrors, where they serve an inimitably crisp martini as well as a luminous ice green beauty of a gimlet, both with little counter glasses for the overflow. Divine. If someone told me they had only one night to spend in Hollywood, I'd send them to Musso's.

NIC'S

453 N. CANON DR. (AT LITTLE SANTA MONICA), BEVERLY HILLS (310) 550-5707. OPEN MON.–SAT., 5 P.M.–MIDNIGHT OR 1 A.M.; CLOSED SUN. FULL BAR. ALL AGES IN RESTAURANT; 21 AND OVER IN THE BAR. NO COVER. FOOD (ECLECTIC). $$.

A tony Beverly Hills restaurant with a welcoming front bar serving fruit-infused cocktails they call martinis. While you and I may know that the only fruit that goes in a martini is an olive, you may find yourself softening when you taste vodka infused with pomegranates. There's live music several nights a week and a pretty patio in back, where, should you choose to dine, you will be rewarded with renowned LA chef Larry Nicola's often-excellent fusion cuisine. In an area with a dearth of neighborly drinking spots, Nic's is most welcome.

NORMANDIE ROOM

8737 SANTA MONICA BLVD. (BETWEEN LA CIENEGA AND SAN VINCENTE, AT HANCOCK), WEST HOLLYWOOD (310) 659-6204. OPEN DAILY, 5 P.M.–2 A.M. FULL BAR. 21 AND OVER. NO COVER. NO FOOD. $$.

While the Normandie Room's cast-aluminum signage makes it look like a design firm from the outside, within it is a friendly, mostly lesbian and gay bar, with a small pool table tucked in an asymmetrical nook, a casual let's-watch-the-game atmosphere, and floor-to-ceiling windows that let you check out this particularly bustling section of Santa Monica Boulevard. A good neighborhood spot.

NORTH

8029 SUNSET BLVD. (A HALF BLOCK EAST OF CRESCENT HEIGHTS), WEST HOLLYWOOD (323) 654-1313. OPEN MON.–SAT., 6 P.M.–2 A.M.; SUN., 7 P.M.–2 A.M. FULL BAR. 21 AND OVER. NO COVER. FOOD (CALIFORNIA-ECLECTIC). $$.

The entryway to North is so luminous, I always feel as though I'm walking into Tiffany's and any minute a guard is going to tell me to get my grubby hands off the counters. Downstairs, the bar and restaurant say Scandinavian: pale woods, minimalist chandeliers, slate floors, and a full wall of etched glass through which a "permanent sunset" glints cleanly off the copper bar. Complementing the beautiful room is a young and styling crowd, sipping the latest top-shelf vodkas, nibbling baby lamb chops, and reveling in the fact that, while they may have been hard-core partiers just a few years back, their production deals did indeed come through and everything is turning out better than all right.

NOVA EXPRESS

426 N. FAIRFAX AVE. (BETWEEN MELROSE AND BEVERLY), LOS ANGELES (323) 658-7533. OPEN DAILY, 5 P.M.–4 A.M. BEER AND WINE ONLY. ALL AGES. NO COVER. FOOD (PIZZA). $.

Though an argument can be made that sci-fi geeks already rule the world, I'll believe it when you can no longer get a seat at Nova Express, a techno/gonzo spot that is part coffeehouse, part reading room, part departure pod. Named after the William Burroughs novel, the dark tinged-with-day-glo-paint room is full of intergalactic furnishings, comic books, and lots of futuristic nooks in which to ingest the latest issue of *Hate*, a pulp paperback, or a slice of pizza.

OIL CAN HARRY'S

11502 Ventura Blvd. (between Tujunga and Colfax), Studio City (818) 760-9749. www.oilcanharrysla.com. Open Tues., Thurs.–Sat., 8 p.m.–2 a.m.; closed, Sun., Mon., and Wed. Full bar. 21 and over. Cover, $3–$5. No food. $$.

Ever wonder about that 1890s gent in the top hat, high on an old black-and-white billboard on Ventura? He's Oil Can Harry, the mascot for a gay country-and-western dance club in Studio City that attracts a local, somewhat older crowd and anyone else who wants to cowboy up and dance. (Two left boots? Take a free lesson, Tuesday and Thursday at 7:45 P.M.) Thursday is an especially chick-friendly night, with women getting down to the Dixie Chicks and Shania; Saturday, it's retro-disco, with all the Donna Summer, Bee Gees, and Gloria Gaynor you can bump to.

OPIUM DEN

1608 Cosmo St. (one block south of Hollywood Blvd.), Hollywood (323) 466-7800. Open Sun.–Thurs., 9 p.m.–2 a.m., Fri. and Sat., 10 p.m.–2 a.m. Full bar. 21 and over. Cover varies. No food. $$.

Years ago, this space was called the Gaslight, and night crawlers loved everything about it, from the crummy-alley entrance to the anything-goes booking policy, from the always-packed patio to the bad behavior by the minute. Then the place changed its name and cleaned up a wee bit, though thankfully not enough to take out the nastiness. The crowd is still Hollywood, young, slightly smutty, and happy to do anything so long as they don't have to go home; the music/scene is still manic—deejays spinning rare grooves/acid jazz, funk or hip-hop, or live band lineups, usually punk, garage, and rock.

THE PALMS

8572 SANTA MONICA BLVD. (ONE BLOCK WEST OF LA CIENEGA), WEST HOLLYWOOD (310) 652-6188. OPEN DAILY, 2 P.M.–2 A.M. FULL BAR. 21 AND OVER. COVER AFTER 8 P.M., $3–$5. NO FOOD. $.

Way back in 1972, I am told, there were very few girl bars in Los Angeles. Enter the Palms, which turns 30 next year, a reliably cozy, mostly lesbian bar. While the Palms is not distinguished in terms of looks—deep-dark mirrored bar, small dance floor, pool table—the bartenders and clients are very friendly, the deejays will play what you want to hear, and the mood is almost always festive. In addition to weekly dance nights (funk, retro, eighties), the Sunday afternoon Beer Bust and barbecue on the spacious patio, and the occasional lineup of lesbian comedians, the Palms gets into the swing of things with pajama parties, a Halloween costume contest, and all sorts of festivities for Gay Pride Day. A good neighborhood spot that attracts folks from as far away as San Diego.

PINOT HOLLYWOOD

1448 GOWER ST. (AT SUNSET), HOLLYWOOD (323) 461-8800. OPEN MON.–SAT., 11:30 A.M.–1 A.M.; CLOSED SUN. FULL BAR. 21 AND OVER IN THE BAR. NO COVER. FOOD (FRENCH-CALIFORNIA). $$.

One of Joachim Splichal's gazillion restaurants, wrapped around a bar as intimate as a sanctuary—the sort of urbane and comfortable setting where you can conduct business or flirt like mad with equal ease. There's also a romantic lounge, where you can sink into an overstuffed sofa, order a few nibbles from the bar menu, and warm your feet by the fire. Go when you're in the mood for peace and plenty.

THE PLAYROOM

836 N. HIGHLAND AVE. (ONE BLOCK NORTH OF MELROSE), HOLLYWOOD (323) 461-8301. OPEN MON., WED., FRI., AND SAT.; TIMES VARY BY EVENING; CALL FOR INF. FULL BAR. 21 AND OVER; 18 AND OVER WED. COVER VARIES. NO FOOD. $$.

If any club illustrates the paradigm that LA venues are places with liquor licenses where promoters can host weekly events, it's the Playroom (formerly the Probe). Done up in plush purple and black, with a big performance room (and a small VIP area), the Playroom is currently hosting the hottest Friday-night club in town, seventies and eighties glitz-and-glam revival **Cherry** (for information: (213) 896-9099, or www.clubcherry.com), with gal-and-guy go-go dancers, and deejays Mike Messex and Joseph Brooks spinning Blondie/Bowie/Joan Jett et al. and whipping the crowd into a libidinous frenzy. On Monday, it's **Scream,** a raucous, very hot scene with live rock bands and deejay Coyote Shivers getting the girlies weak in the knees. (For information: (818) 763-8552.)

POLO LOUNGE

BEVERLY HILLS HOTEL, 9641 SUNSET BLVD. (AT COLDWATER CANYON), BEVERLY HILLS (310) 276-2251. OPEN DAILY, 7 A.M.– 1:30 A.M. ALL AGES; 21 AND OVER IN THE BAR. FOOD (CONTINENTAL). $$$.

Some places are all about make-believe, and for me, the Polo Lounge—heck, the whole Beverly Hills Hotel—is one of them. Are my legs long enough to lounge decoratively by the pool? Sadly, no. Are my holdings plush enough to let me rent a bungalow for the season? I don't even have a savings account. Yet, on occasion, I feel the desire to pretend I do, which is when I put on my Emilio Pucci, take up residence in the splendid woody bar, and, ensconced in one of the enormous booths with a few similarly fabulous-for-the-evening friends, pretend that the most effort I ever need exert is the signing of the chit.

POWER HOUSE

1714 N. HIGHLAND AVE. (A HALF BLOCK NORTH OF HOLLYWOOD), HOLLYWOOD (323) 463-9438. OPEN DAILY, 10 A.M.–2 A.M. FULL BAR. 21 AND OVER. NO COVER. NO FOOD. $.

A dark little dive in the shadows of Hollywood Boulevard, visited mainly by folks who will never be ready for their close-ups. A good place on a hot day for a cold beer, as it's never crowded and no one is inclined to talk your ear off. That may all change soon: since it sits directly across the street from a new 1-million-square-foot entertainment and shopping complex, the Power House may soon find itself the busiest little dive in Hollywood.

THE QUEEN MARY NIGHT CLUB

12449 VENTURA BLVD. (BETWEEN LAUREL CANYON AND COLDWATER CANYON, AT WHITSETT), NORTH HOLLYWOOD (818) 506-5619. WWW.QUEENMARYNIGHTCLUB.COM. OPEN TUES.–SUN., 8:30 P.M.–2 A.M.; CLOSED MON. FULL BAR. 21 AND OVER. COVER VARIES. NO FOOD. $$.

Don't feel like driving five hours to Vegas? Check out the drag Vegas-style reviews at the Queen Mary, where the dancers have been strutting and stripping and shimmying for 40 years. All kinds of folks make the scene—gays and straights; cross-dressers and guys in drag decked out as everything from showgirl to secretary, nurse to newscaster. You can check out the three-plus-hour (!) shows Friday to Sunday or the karaoke other nights, or simply hang in the back bar and boogie on the two tiny dance floors. Certainly the only place of its kind in the Valley.

RAGE

8911 SANTA MONICA BLVD. (ONE BLOCK EAST OF SAN VINCENTE), WEST HOLLYWOOD (310) 652-7055. OPEN DAILY, 2 P.M.–2 A.M.; SOME NIGHTS UNTIL 3:30 A.M. FULL BAR. 21 AND OVER (THURS., 18 AND OVER). COVER VARIES. FOOD (BURGERS). $$.

Imagine the prototypical gay disco portrayed in the movies, with the floor packed with good-looking guys in muscle shirts, who are pumping and sweating to loud music. See it? Now add some chicks, vary the music (alternative, KROQ-type rock, Latin), throw in a restaurant, half-price drinks every night until 8 P.M., and a location in the middle of West Hollywood.... You get the picture.

THE RED GARTER

2536 LINCOLN BLVD. (JUST NORTH OF WASHINGTON), SANTA MONICA (310) 306-8300. OPEN DAILY, 10 A.M.–2 P.M. FULL BAR, 21 AND OVER. NO COVER. NO FOOD. $.

Red-and-gold velvet wallpaper, Merle Haggard and Hank Williams on the jukebox, and working Joes shooting pool and drinking ice-cold beer. No need to dandy it up further than that; stop in when you're in the mood for American.

RED LION TAVERN

2366 GLENDALE BLVD. (AT SILVERLAKE), SILVERLAKE (323) 662-5337. OPEN DAILY, 11 A.M.–2 A.M. FULL BAR. 21 AND OVER. NO COVER. FOOD (GERMAN). $$.

A Bavarian beer hall shrunk to Silverlake proportions. With old wood paneling that's soaked up the smell of beer, big blonde barmaids wearing dirndls, and an accordion player oom-pah-pah-ing in the corner, the place is comfortable and hokey. Which doesn't mean you'll be marooned with a bunch of Germans reminiscing about Willy Brandt. While there's always a chummy assortment of florid-faced Europeans at the bar, the Red Lion also attracts sizable clots of local artists and musicians, and anyone who appreciates enormous steins of Wacsteiner and Spaten, icy shots of Jagermeister on tap, and trencherman portions of spaetzle and bratwurst. Above the downstairs bar is another bar, a spooky little grotto where about six can drink comfortably. Beyond that is a large patio, with tables that'll fit a crowd, an overhead carving of lederhosen-clad drinkers clanking steins, and a sign pointing the way to Berlin, "Sister City of Los Angeles." This is a great place to bring a group on a summer night, and one of the very few spots in Los Angeles where you actually feel you're in a German beer garden.

REGAL BILTMORE, GALLERY BAR

506 S. GRAND AVE. (AT 5TH ST.), DOWNTOWN LA (213) 624-1011, EXT. 1206. OPEN DAILY, 4:30 P.M.–1:45 A.M. FULL BAR. 21 AND OVER. NO COVER. NO FOOD. $$.

What a wacky place the Regal Biltmore Hotel is, baroque in decor, just tatty around the edges, and host to seemingly every LA convention and awards show, including a recent PEN West dinner that stretched into the five-hour mark, at which point a bunch of rogue journalists decamped for the Gallery Bar. The room itself is smashing, with burnished gold walls and Deco inlays that have been there since the 1920s (when the bar was called the Gold Room, and where, despite Prohibition, the local mucky-mucks imbibed; legend has it that, when G-men got too close, getaways were made via a secret passage). Romantic? Perhaps, though the bar is just as likely filled (as it was that night) with tourists watching *Friends* on a TV behind the bar. Still, if you're downtown, it's just about the swankiest spot to grab a drink.

RESIDUALS

11042 VENTURA BLVD. (AT VINELAND), STUDIO CITY (818) 761-8301. OPEN MON.-FRI., 11:30 A.M.–2 A.M.; SAT. AND SUN., 4 P.M.–2 A.M. FULL BAR. 21 AND OVER. NO COVER. FOOD (BURGERS). $.

A large, friendly bar that caters to actors and others who work (or would like to work) at the nearby studios. Ultracasual, with a sort of suburban look and feel, Residuals has live jazz on Friday, rhythm and blues on Saturday, and karaoke on Sunday. But it's not really the sort of place one goes to be entertained—it's better for sitting with fellow performers and, while working through a basket of free popcorn and a few mugs of beer, conspiring to get one's head shot to David Kelley.

THE ROOM

1626 N. CAHUENGA BLVD. (AT HOLLYWOOD; ENTRANCE IN BACK ALLEY), HOLLYWOOD (323) 462-7196. OPEN SUN.-THURS., 7 P.M.–2 A.M.; FRI. AND SAT., 8 P.M.–2 A.M. FULL BAR. 21 AND OVER. NO COVER. NO FOOD. $.

If you haven't been to The Room in a while, you're in for a little surprise: what was, at the height of the lounge's resurgence, the most Sinatra-steeped hipster bar in Hollywood (and a place where I personally spent several hundred hours) has added a serious music and dance scene to its allure. With the same hidden entrance (through the alley in back) and the same great room—almost pitch-black, with a classically beautiful bar and big booths—The Room now hosts serious deejays spinning funk, soul, hip-hop, acid jazz, and old soul most nights. Well-done both ways, and an absolute must for anyone on the Hollywood bar tour.

THE ROOM S.M.

1325 SANTA MONICA BLVD. (AT 14TH ST.; ENTRANCE IN REAR), SANTA MONICA (310) 458-0707. OPEN SUN., TUES.-THURS., 7 P.M.–2 A.M.; FRI. AND SAT., 8 P.M.–2 A.M.; CLOSED MON. FULL BAR. 21 AND OVER. NO COVER. NO FOOD. $.

What the original The Room in Hollywood was—a hipster bar as friendly as a British pub, thanks to its owners, Welshman Jeremy Thomas and Brit Ashley Joyce—The Room S.M. is. Though the space is four times the size of its shotgun predecessor, otherwise the new Room resembles the old: it's terrifically dark, the music is sexy (deep house, soul, Sinatra), and it's got the same semicircular booths and the same friendly bartenders ready to tap you a pint. A godsend for Santa Monicans craving both a neighborhood pub and a little lounge life.

THE ROOST

3100 LOS FELIZ BLVD. (TWO BLOCKS EAST OF GLENFELIZ), LOS FELIZ (323) 664-7272. OPEN DAILY, 10 A.M.–2 A.M. FULL BAR. 21 AND OVER. NO COVER. NO FOOD. $.

A cavernous Atwater lounge that used to be so underpopulated I wondered how they stayed in business. It has now been somewhat colonized by nearby Silverlakers starved for a large bar they can call their own on the weekends. Otherwise, this unassuming place puts one in mind of the Midwest, with inexpensive drinks, free baskets of popcorn, a pool table, friendly/surly gal bartenders, and a local game playing at all times on the mounted TV. Not a whole lot of ambiance and they like it that way, thank you very much. If you find yourself in the area, and every place else is packed, odds are you'll find a seat here.

ROXY

9009 SUNSET BLVD. (AT DOHENY), WEST HOLLYWOOD (310) 276-2222. OPEN NIGHTLY, FROM 8 P.M. "UNTIL THE BANDS ARE DONE." FULL BAR. ALL AGES. COVER VARIES. FOOD (AMERICAN). $$.

Everything here is black—walls, floors, fixtures—some say to cover the accumulated dirt that comes with 26 years of showcasing rock 'n' roll, from the Clash to Springsteen, Bob Marley to Pee Wee Herman (who performed *Pee-Wee's Playhouse* here). Though the lineups tend to be less celebrated these days, the Roxy is still all about music: the bar is small, the PAs are huge, and all focus is on the stage, where up to five bands a night thrash it out. Rock and punk, rhythm and blues and hillbilly, surf-rock and pop—you name it, they play it here. The crowd tends toward hair farmers, stud-muffins, and people who still care a lot about denim.

THE RUBY

7070 HOLLYWOOD BLVD. (AT LA BREA), HOLLYWOOD (323) 467-7070. OPEN WED.–SUN., 9 P.M.–3 A.M.; CLOSED MON. AND TUES. FULL BAR. 18 AND OVER. COVER VARIES. NO FOOD. $$.

This massive venue in the disco tradition (strobe lights and smoke machines) hosts various weekly clubs, including the long-running **Perversion** (Thursday), with each of the Ruby's three rooms spinning different sounds (industrial/electronica, New Wave/showtunes, goth/dark eighties, respectively) for a young, quasi-goth crowd. There's also **Bang!** (Saturday), with the ripped-fishnets and dog-collar crew getting down to sixties and seventies tunes in the front room, eighties and nineties in the main room, and the "sounds of the future" in the back. The sort of place where you wander around, dance a little, and sit on a speaker/collapse in a corner until closing time, when you hit the street with the sense memory of the bass still buzzing your cheeks and the inside of your ears.

RUDOLPHO'S

2500 RIVERSIDE DR. (AT FLETCHER), SILVERLAKE (323) 669-1226. OPEN MON., WED., FRI., AND SAT. NIGHTS, 9 P.M.–2 A.M. (DRAGSTRIP 66, UNTIL 3 A.M.). FULL BAR. 21 AND OVER. COVER, $6–$10. NO FOOD. $$.

A local Mexican restaurant by day/mostly gay salsa scene (with dance lessons available, Monday, 8 to 9 P.M.) several nights a week. Rudolpho's is also celebrated for its be-bop/rockabilly evenings (every third and fourth Friday of the month) and, most notably, **Dragstrip 66** (for information: (323) 969-2596; www.dragstrip66.com), the come-as-you-are-or-want-to-be drag scene held the second Saturday of each month. There's the usual assortment of Catholic schoolgirls (most better-looking than the real thing) and fab/drab divas, though many choose not to dress, happy simply to watch and dance to whatever wackiness the deejays are spinning (anything from Marlene Dietrich to Neil Diamond, sitcom jingles to Bow Wow Wow). The crush on the patio (and I do mean crush: claustrophobes, beware) reminds me of some fabulous gay bash on Fire Island. And speaking of crowds, DG66 is always packed by 11 P.M., so if you don't want to stand in line, you need either to get there early or to dress with such dazzle/big balls that the crowd parts before you.

SAM'S HOFBRAU

1751 East Olympic Blvd. (one block north of Alameda), Downtown LA (213) 623-3989. www.samshofbrau.com. Open daily, 10 a.m.–2 a.m. Full bar. 21 and over. No cover. Food (sandwiches). $$.

A large strip bar frequented by truckers and day laborers and those who need things harder than they can get in Hollywood, Sam's Hofbrau feels more Rust Belt than Downtown. In other words, this is not a gentleman's club, but a strip bar, with lots of hooting and hollering, plenty of loud rock 'n' roll, some very game girls, and the occasional amateur night. Dozens of tables, a spacious, U-shaped platform that assures dancers maximum exposure, and a long, candy-apple red bar can conspire to keep you at Sam's a little longer than you'd planned. Don't feel like making the trek downtown? Check out their splashy Web site.

SHUTTERS, LOBBY BAR

Shutters Hotel, 1 Pico Blvd. (at Ocean), Santa Monica (310) 458-0030. Open daily, 6 p.m.–2 a.m. Full bar. All ages. No cover. Food (American, available from 1 Pico). $$$.

The first thing I think when I walk into Shutters is, I bet these people paid a lot for their clothes. Casually reclining on plush couches, the sartorially gifted Westside crowd is mixed in equal proportion with expense-account tourists willing to pay for the water view. Try to snag one of the five outdoor tables, where you can see the sunset or, if it's darker, watch the reflectors on the shoes of the runners on the bike path and listen to the ocean.

SILVERLAKE LOUNGE/FOLD

2906 SUNSET BLVD. (AT PARKMAN), SILVERLAKE (323) 666-2407. WWW.LOOP.COM/~FOLD. OPEN TUES.–THURS., 9 P.M.–2 A.M. FULL BAR. 21 AND OVER. COVER VARIES. NO FOOD. $.

A fairly dingy drinking man's bar that lets the Silverlake squad do their thing several nights a week—that thing being taping a little tinsel around the eaves and giving up-and-coming acts and touring groups a jewel-box-tiny stage on which to thrash it out. Music can be unexpectedly superb, as was a lineup of Japanese all-girl bubble-gum pop groups that energized the room with goofy ferocity. A sweet little scene, thanks to the bookers' store of fresh ideas and the ready-for-anything audience the Fold attracts.

SKY BAR

MONDRIAN HOTEL, 8440 SUNSET BLVD. (ONE BLOCK EAST OF LA CIENEGA), WEST HOLLYWOOD (323) 848-6025. OPEN DAILY, 11 A.M.–2 A.M. GUESTS ONLY POLICY CAN BE FLEXIBLE. FULL BAR. 21 AND OVER. NO COVER. FOOD (EXPANDED BAR MENU). $$.

While I admire the room itself—an elevated, woody affair that looks like a cross between a Maine camp and a meetinghouse—and while the nearby flush-with-the-patio pool is an almost unimaginable blue, with (if you go for that sort of thing) a postcard view to the beach, I cannot say I like the Sky Bar very much. Its enforced exclusivity (guests only . . . and those beautiful/rich/slick enough to get around that rule) feels like being stuck at a party with people you don't really like. Add overpriced drinks served in the kind of plastic cups you rinse with at the dentist (something about drunks and glass and swimming pools), blasé bartenders, and door guys who've turned to stone from listening to all the lame-o stories of desperadoes trying to wax their way in, and I can't see any reason why you'd want to drink here.

THE SMELL

247 S. MAIN ST. (AT 3RD), DOWNTOWN LA (213) 625-4325. OPEN WED.–SAT., HOURS VARY. NO BAR. ALL AGES. COVER VARIES. NO FOOD. $.

A storefront-cum-art gallery/nightclub, showcasing punk/garage/experimental bands blowing through town and/or releasing CDs, and the sort of valuable/hostile/up-in-the-ether sounds and performances that demand the space and humor of a high-minded/low-rent venue. The crowd is Downtown, unruly and appreciative.

SMOG CUTTER

864 N. VIRGIL AVE. (AT NORMAL), SILVERLAKE (323) 667-9832. OPEN DAILY, NOON–2 A.M. FULL BAR. 21 AND OVER. NO COVER. NO FOOD. $.

This Silverlake dive rose to prominence several years ago when they began hosting (Wednesday to Sunday) a fun and funny karaoke scene: slackers singing "I Am Woman" (guys only) and the theme from *The Love Boat* in a tiny room with one sorry pool table, bottom-shelf liquor, and a hostess named Sunshine. Yes, there are hostesses—pretty Thai women wearing silk wraps, asking whether you are having a nice time. The crowd is very mixed—day laborers, local Bohos, Westsiders who find the scene a silly departure. And it can be. It can also be smushed, a tinderbox of alcohol-fueled emotions (thrown punches, tearful contrition), and a little shabby.

SPACELAND

1717 SILVERLAKE BLVD. (A HALF MILE NORTH OF SUNSET, AT EFFIE), SILVERLAKE (213) 833-2843/AFTER 8 P.M., (323) 661-4380. WWW.CLUBSPACELAND.COM. OPEN MON.–SAT., 6 P.M.– 2 A.M. FULL BAR. 21 AND OVER. COVER VARIES. FOOD (MIDDLE EASTERN). $$.

If, as was proclaimed back in the early nineties, Silverlake was the new Seattle, it owes much of that distinction to Spaceland, a club that gave alternative acts a legitimate stage and Bohos a place to show off their Goodwill gear. Almost a decade later, Spaceland maintains solid and eclectic bookings but has a slightly spiffier look. While the downstairs bar and stage area are moderately raw, the high-tech upstairs lounge looks like a 1970s set designer's wet dream: lots of smoked black glass and gleaming chrome, satellite dishes on the ceiling, and a bar that looks as if it might have the power to suck you into hyperspace. If you have any interest in what's going on in alternative/rock/garage music, Spaceland should be at the top of your list.

SPORTSMEN'S LODGE MUDDY MOOSE BAR AND GRILL

12833 VENTURA BLVD. (AT COLDWATER CANYON), STUDIO CITY (818) 755-5000. OPEN DAILY, 11 A.M.–11:30 P.M. FULL BAR. 21 AND OVER. NO COVER. FOOD (AMERICAN). $$.

Yes, there's a bar in this massive hotel/conference complex, and it's exactly the sort of place you'd expect to find at any hotel/conference complex across this great land: big, impersonal, with overly conditioned air and too much ice in the drinks. The sort of place where, sitting at the bar, I narrowly avoid an existential crash, observing the people having affairs, the overweight conventioneers, the bitter divorcee, the dogged solo drinker. When the live music starts (7:30 P.M.)—usually top forties and oldies groups from around the Valley—I really plummet, now having to also absorb the crisis that is the band. Ow. And yet, a ray of hope in the form of salsa on Friday nights, including such inestimable players as Johnny Polanco y Su Conjunto Amistad, which brings out lots of happy dancing people. Phew.

THE SPOT LIGHT CLUB

1601 CAHUENGA BLVD. (ONE BLOCK SOUTH OF HOLLYWOOD) HOLLYWOOD (323) 467-2425. OPEN DAILY, 6 A.M.–2 A.M. FULL BAR. 21 AND OVER. NO COVER. NO FOOD. $.

You can't miss the Spot Light: it's the place on the corner of Cahuenga and Ivar outside of which there are usually a few folks gunning for a fight/slumped against the wall/looking as though they've just plummeted to earth and have yet to find their bearings. Inside, it's a sweet little room lit with party lights and possessing lots and lots (and lots) of local color. A rugged spot to spend the afternoon with a fellow diehard.

STONEWALL GOURMET COFFEE

8717 SANTA MONICA BLVD. (AT WESTBOURNE), WEST HOLLYWOOD (310) 659-8009. WWW.STONEWALLINC.COM. OPEN DAILY, 7 A.M.–10 P.M. AND LATER. NO ALCOHOL. FOOD (COFFEE AND PASTRIES). $.

This coffeehouse (exposed-brick variety) in the heart of Boys Town becomes a rollicking bingo palace on Thursday, starting at 8:30 P.M., when various drag queens and celebrities shout out the numbers, with profits benefiting various charities. A lot of fun: if the decibel level doesn't keep you awake (the action can get loud and raucous), the good coffee and treats will.

SUNSET ROOM

1430 CAHUENGA BLVD. (A HALF BLOCK SOUTH OF SUNSET), HOLLYWOOD (323) 463-0004. OPEN TUES.–THURS., 7 P.M.–11:30 P.M.; FRI. AND SAT., 7 P.M.–2 A.M., THOUGH IF DINNER CROWD IS VERY BUSY, BAR-ONLY PATRONS WILL NOT BE ADMITTED UNTIL 9:30 P.M. FULL BAR. 21 AND OVER. NO COVER FOR BAR; $15 COVER FOR CLUB. FOOD (ECLECTIC). $$$.

I put off going to Sunset Room for months, as I'd heard so many awful things about the place: the limos and scads of conspicuous cash being flashed, the velvet rope and nasty bartenders, the "look at me!" clientele. Well, it's simply not as bad as all that. Yes, the enormous club/bar/restaurant stylistically marries industrial with British Empire, with a few ferns and a little bad art tossed on top; yes, a shot of Patron costs $12 (and dinner will set you back an easy $70). But the acoustics are great, with mellow jazz filling the room like so much warm water, and the appointments are nothing less than sumptuous, with every highback booth and club chair deep enough to sleep in. There's also a big patio with a roaring fire and its own bar (where, if I had a spare $200, I'd invite a few friends for a few drinks); a separate dance club where, Thursday to Saturday, deejays spin ambient, rhythm and blues, a little Brazilian; a VIP room with its own bar; and, if that's not exclusive enough, private cabañas for doing god-knows-what within yards of the traffic on Cahuenga. Sunset Room has been a place to be for about a year, but I doubt it will remain so, the popularity of a place like Sunset Room being, like the lovelies who inhabit it for a season, evanescent and easily supplanted by the next monument to excess. Which I don't think is a bad thing: if Sunset Room took itself a little less seriously, I'd recommend its ultraluxe in a second.

TEMPEST

7323 SANTA MONICA BLVD. (BETWEEN LA BREA AND FAIRFAX), WEST HOLLYWOOD (323) 850-5115. OPEN NIGHTLY, 8:30 P.M.–2 A.M. FULL BAR. 21 AND OVER, WITH OCCASIONAL 18 AND OVER NIGHTS. COVER $5–$10. FOOD (CALIFORNIA-ITALIAN). $$.

A small Italian-by-way-of-LA restaurant that turns into an ever-changing series of dance/performance clubs Thursday through Sunday nights. They revolve so fast that I hesitate to list what's currently there, as it probably won't be by the time you read this. Two recent happenings: the smashing revival of Rodney Bingenheimer's English Disco, which drew thousands of birds in white boots and boys on scooters, and Absythe, an every-other-Sunday goth club. (More information: (323) 860-6663, or www.fiendish.org.)

TEMPLE BAR

1026 WILSHIRE BLVD. (BETWEEN 10TH AND 11TH), SANTA MONICA (310) 393-6611. WWW.TEMPLEBARLIVE.COM. OPEN NIGHTLY, 6 P.M.–2 A.M. FULL BAR. 21 AND OVER. COVER, $3–$10. FOOD (CARIBBEAN). $$.

There's a Buddha theme going on in this sexy/exotic, candlelit lounge, but the main thing the multitudes worship is the live music, performed mostly by black, Latino, and Native American groups (Sioux activist-poet-actor-bluesman John Trudell plays here). With an emphasis on funk, hip-hop, and rhythm and blues, the room can get tight, and the music is often so hard and mighty, it passes the "good show" litmus test: corpuscles throbbing in rhythm hours after the music's ended. Strong martini menu, and enough spicy/salty snacks (crab cakes, calamari, jerk chicken) to keep the indefatigable crowd powered through the last song.

360°

6290 SUNSET BLVD. (AT VINE), HOLLYWOOD (323) 871-2995. OPEN NIGHTLY, 6 P.M.–2 A.M.; CLUBS OPEN AT 10 P.M. FULL BAR. 21 AND OVER. NO COVER. FOOD (AMERICAN-ECLECTIC). $$.

Up, up, and away, atop an office tower on Sunset and Vine, is the ultrasmooth restaurant and bar 360°. Sure, the Continental cuisine is great (really great: try the steak) and the bar scene pumping (there's a very popular gay club, **Beige,** on Tuesday, and a hip-hop/funk/rare groove night, **Straight Up,** every Thursday). But the real coup is the altitude. With views from Downtown to the beach, the lounge is a prime place to kick back, sip a cocktail, and transcend the gritty gravitational pull of Hollywood.

THREE OF CLUBS

1123 N. VINE ST. (A HALF BLOCK NORTH OF SANTA MONICA), HOLLYWOOD (323) 462-6441. OPEN NIGHTLY, 8 P.M.–2 A.M. FULL BAR. 21 AND OVER. NO COVER. NO FOOD. $$.

I love Three of Clubs' look, from the beautifully lit New York–style front bar and lounge (where, if you're lucky, there will be a little Sinatra playing low), to the great-for-mingling main room, where there are lots of chairs and couches that make the place feel like a party in someone's giant living room, and where the fuel comes from live music or a deejay playing good funk. The only problem I ever had with Three of Clubs was a few years back, at the height of the lounge scene, when it became so painfully the place to be that the door guys got big heads, the scene inside got a little frantic, and people who'd been hanging there for years said, "Later." But Three of Clubs has mellowed, the door guys have sweetened, and the welcome mat's back. So's the crowd.

TIKI THEATER

5462 SANTA MONICA BLVD. (ONE BLOCK EAST OF WESTERN), HOLLYWOOD (323) 462-0345. OPEN 24 HOURS. NO ALCOHOL. 21 AND OVER. COVER, $8. NO FOOD. $$.

If you think you've seen it all, check out the Tiki Theater, a crummy live-sex-show theater that is at once so stark and so sad, the last guy I went there with started to cry. Here's what we saw: an overweight, middle-aged Bulgarian woman stripping on the small stage, wriggling out of her winter clothes and support hose until she was down to a woolen muffler. Fully exposed and shivering, she did a little shimmy from side to side while tapping her watch and holding it to her ear, checking (it appeared) to see if she actually existed in time. For this, she earned $7 from the assembled, mostly dead-eyed men with their trench coats in their laps.

TIKI-TI

4427 SUNSET BLVD. (BETWEEN HILLHURST AND FOUNTAIN), SILVERLAKE (323) 669-9381. OPEN WED.–SAT., 6 P.M.–2 A.M.; CLOSED SUN.–TUES. FULL BAR. 21 AND OVER. NO COVER. NO FOOD. $.

A tiny A-frame hut, the Tiki-Ti feels as though it washed up whole from the shores of Hawaii. Inside, the palm-thatched room is packed with 1,000 island geegaws, including one desiccated blowfish whose name defies pronunciation, especially after you imbibe a few of the dozens of rum concoctions blended up by the 80-something-year-old owner, who opened the place in 1961. (Bonus: because Tiki-Ti's owner-operated, you can smoke.) The crowd runs to local kids, the college crew, old dudes, and married couples—everyone who appreciates a sweet little hideaway. The only problem with the Tiki-Ti is, the place is so tiny, it's sometimes impossible to get in the door.

TOM BERGIN'S

840 S. FAIRFAX AVE. (BETWEEN WILSHIRE AND OLYMPIC), LOS ANGELES (323) 936-7151. WWW.TOMBERGINS.COM. OPEN SUN.-THURS., 4 P.M.-2 A.M.; FRI. AND SAT., 12 P.M.-2 A.M. FULL BAR. 21 AND OVER. NO COVER. FOOD (IRISH-AMERICAN). $$

If you overlook the thousands of shamrocks plastered to the ceiling, and ignore the Rod Stewart replays on the sound system, Tom Bergin's is a pleasant, low-key watering hole, the sort of place you find as easily in suburban New Jersey as just south of Wilshire. The bartenders are affable, there's a warming Irish stew made with Guinness, and the customers, mostly business people, seem kind. Not a hip place and not trying to be.

TOMMY TANG'S

7313 MELROSE AVE. (BETWEEN LA BREA AND FAIRFAX, AT FULLER), HOLLYWOOD (323) 937-5733. WWW.TOMMYTANGS.NET. OPEN DAILY, 11 A.M.-1 P.M. BEER AND WINE ONLY. ALL AGES. NO COVER. FOOD (THAI). $$

This wonderful Thai restaurant has a special on Tuesday: beautiful boy waiters in drag. Before you think, "What's next—Belle Aire at the Beef Bowl?" know that Tommy Tang's has been doing this for over a decade, that the "showgirls" are gorgeous *and* efficient in their gowns and corselettes, that everyone from rock stars to families to foodies flocks in on Tuesday, and that the enthusiasm and aggregate temperature soar hotter than that crimson pepper in your cashew chicken.

TRADER VIC'S

BEVERLY-HILTON HOTEL, 9876 WILSHIRE BLVD. (AT SANTA MONICA BLVD.), BEVERLY HILLS (310) 276-6345. OPEN

DAILY, 5 P.M.–1 A.M. FULL BAR. ALL AGES. NO COVER. FOOD (POLYNESIAN-AMERICAN). $$$.

Most people have been to (or at least have heard of) Trader Vic's, a chain of Polynesian restaurants and bars usually found in hotels. This branch does not deviate from the others in form or decor: the room is junglelike, the food runs to shrimp/coconut combinations, the majority of customers are tourists, and the powerful rum cocktails, served in "skulls," are so massive and so deceptively sweet that, before you know it, you cannot possibly get behind the wheel of a car. I know someone who deliberately arranged to meet a potential lover at Trader Vic's, on the theory that one of them would get so sloshed, he or she would have no choice but to escort the other home. It worked.

TRAXX

800 N. ALAMEDA ST. (IN UNION STATION), DOWNTOWN LA (213) 625-1999. OPEN MON.–FRI., 11:30 A.M.–9 P.M.; SAT., 5:30 P.M.–10 P.M.; CLOSED SUN. FULL BAR. 21 AND OVER. NO COVER. NO FOOD. $$.

This posh Deco bar has a cool paint job (really), cool lighting, and Billie Holiday on the sound system. Because it's in the lobby of Union Station, it's also the perfect place to watch humanity in transit: Japanese teens en route to San Francisco, weary Midwest tourists consulting maps, multiply pierced Seattle slackers with their dogs on a rope leash. Even better: go get a drink late at night, when the great and gorgeous station is all but empty. One minus: the loos are allllllllll the way on the other side of the station. One plus: should you need to ditch your date/change your life, there's a train leaving every few minutes.

TROUBADOUR

9081 Santa Monica Blvd. (at Doheny), West Hollywood (310) 276-6168. Open nightly, 8 p.m.–2 a.m. Full bar. All ages. Cover varies. Food (hamburgers). $$.

A seasoned rock club (open since 1957) that wears its age well. It's a big wooden box of a place, with high ceilings, a "VIP balcony," and two bars, one lined with eight-by-tens of all the people who've played there from Elton John to Elvis Costello—literally thousands of rock icons from the sixties on up. The acoustics are loud and clear, and there's no discernible scene to contend with, as the Troubadour's sole unifying property seems to be that everyone here loves music, which visually translates to something as simple as hair care: lots of leonine locks and articulated spikes and stiffly shellacked flips at the Troub. Often the only place touring acts play while in LA, so keep your eye on the listings.

VIDA

1930 Hillhurst Ave. (one block north of Franklin), Los Feliz (323) 660-4446. Open nightly, 6 p.m.–11:30 p.m. Full bar. All ages. No cover. Food (eclectic/Thai). $$.

This Los Feliz restaurant features an emphatically modern and cozy bar. Emphasis on cozy, as the seating area is patterned after a traditional Japanese sushi house, but instead of pretzeling yourself on tatami floor mats, you recline against pillowed banquettes, with low tables just a languid arm's length away. The effect is part opium den, part high-tech utilitarian, as if to say, "Do we really need to work any harder than this at having a good time?" A choice alternative to the Los Feliz lounge scene, and a sweet place to spend a few hours tête-à-tête.

THE VIPER ROOM

8852 SUNSET BLVD. (ONE BLOCK EAST OF SAN VINCENTE), WEST HOLLYWOOD (310) 358-1880. WWW.VIPEROOM.COM. OPEN NIGHTLY, 9 P.M.–2 A.M. FULL BAR. 21 AND OVER. COVER VARIES. NO FOOD. $$.

Goodness gracious, what can I say about the Viper Room that hasn't been written 1,000 times? Surely not that it's co-owned by Johnny Depp; that the new Moderne decor is a knockout; that the schizophrenic booking policy moves from electronica to Latin, go-go to swing, rockabilly to metal without missing a beat; that it's been cool since it opened over a decade ago and shows no sign whatsoever of slowing; that everyone who comes here feels a little better for having done so. But you knew all that.

VIVA CANTINA

900 RIVERSIDE DR. (AT MAIN), BURBANK (818) 845-2425. OPEN DAILY, FROM 11 A.M. "UNTIL PEOPLE LEAVE" (USUALLY AROUND MIDNIGHT). FULL BAR. ALL AGES. NO COVER. FOOD (MEXICAN). $$.

A Mexican bar and restaurant for cowboys (really), in equestrian-friendly Burbank. Hitch your horse to the post outside and come on in for beers and margaritas, Mexican food, and live country bands; fiddlers on Thursday. (Sorry, no dancing.) To really appreciate this western offering, **Sunset Ranch** offers a Moonlight Ride, starting in Griffith Park and taking trails (yes, by moonlight) down to Viva Fresh, where dinner and drinks are served. For more information, call Sunset Ranch at (323) 469-5450.

VODA

1449 2ND ST. (AT BROADWAY), SANTA MONICA (310) 394-9774. OPEN DAILY, 6 P.M.–2 A.M., EXCEPT TUES., 6 P.M.–1 A.M. FULL BAR. 21 AND OVER. NO COVER. FOOD (FONDUE). $$.

Exotic vodka drinks and fondue—who can resist? While a friend gripes that the place is "as cheesy as the fondue, and full of really old guys trying to pick me up," by "old" she means 30 (and when has she not complained about an abundance of pulchritude?). In any case, I like the place. The snug, barely lit room is sort of funky, and the concept of vodka and fondue is so quirky that it's sort of irresistible. For comfort, snag one of the side booths.

VOODOO

4120 W. OLYMPIC BLVD. (AT CRENSHAW), LOS ANGELES (323) 930-9600. WWW.VOODOOLA.COM. NIGHTS VARY, CALL HOTLINE FOR INF.: (310) 851-6335; USUALLY OPEN 9 P.M.–2 A.M. FULL BAR. 21 AND OVER. COVER $10–$20. FOOD (ECLECTIC). $$.

When I first heard of Voodoo and saw what part of town it was in—an uninhabited stretch of east Pico—I figured I'd find a bunch of goth kids biting into blood pellets, in a room tricked out with "black magic" totems. Imagine my surprise when I walked into a sort of goofy/fabulous environment, with plush, postmodern seating areas, sky-boxes overlooking the dance floor, a gleaming copper bar, and a huge patio. The place simply screams "Hold your wrap party here!" There's the occasional live act, more often deejays spinning house/trance, rhythm and blues, or hip-hop. If all this makes you wonder what sort of crew hangs out here, I'm with you. What I can tell you is that they were well dressed, came in all colors, and were celebrating hard.

VYNYL

1650 SCHRADER AVE. (JUST SOUTH OF HOLLYWOOD), HOLLYWOOD (323) 465-7449. WWW.VYNYL.COM. OPEN NIGHTLY, 8 P.M.–2 A.M. FULL BAR. 21 AND OVER. NO FOOD. $$.

An all-about-the-music venue (located in the old Hollywood Moguls space), with a big stage, a swank bar, lots of hi-tone frills, and a great sight line to performers, from Tori Amos to a production of *Hedwig and the Angry Inch*. Bookings range from funk to fusion to folk, record-release parties to awards shows, so if you're into live music, you probably want to keep your eye on what's going on at Vynyl. Several nights a week, the space hosts dance clubs, including **Revival,** early on Sundays (4 P.M. to 11 P.M.), with four deejays furiously spinning a barrage of electronic dance music. Rave on.

WHISKEY BAR

Sunset Marquis Hotel, 1200 Alta Loma Rd. (just south of Sunset), West Hollywood (310) 657-0611. www.srsworldhotels.com. Open nightly, 5:00 p.m.–2:00 a.m. Full bar. 21 and over. No cover. No food. $$.

Men's club meets bad-boy bar in this womb of a room off the lobby of the Sunset Marquis Hotel. With throw-pillow nooks, photos of Mick and Keith in their glory days, generous drinks, and rooms right upstairs, the clientele (actors, agents, New Yorkers, Europeans) feel at liberty to get loose and louche; on one visit, a young Italian assured me he was "the next Al Pacino," licked my underarm, kicked over a beer, and made a grab for the waitress, all in under a minute—the sort of brattiness that's amusing but exhausting, the baby-sitting kind of bar experience. If a friend/business associate is staying upstairs, check out this sexy little bar... though there's always a chance you'll have to wangle your way onto the (sigh) guest list—an atavism the hotels along the Strip have an enduring fondness for.

WHISKY A GOGO

8901 SUNSET BLVD. (ONE BLOCK EAST OF SAN VINCENTE), WEST HOLLYWOOD (310) 652-4202. OPEN NIGHTLY, 8 P.M.–2 A.M. WWW.WHISKEYAGOGO.COM. ALL AGES. FULL BAR. COVER, SUN.–THURS., $10; FRI. AND SAT., $12–$15. FOOD (HAMBURGERS). $$.

The Doors played here and made the Whisky famous, and it's remained one of LA's must-go-go scenes for up-and-coming rockers, their fan base (i.e., friends and family), and diehards who've been hanging here for 30 years. While the Whisky doesn't draw the caliber of acts it once did, bands that harbor a moral soft spot for the small, ratty rock venue will often book a night; e.g., I saw the Ramones play here, and their manic energy was perfectly served by the small, agreeably grungy room.

WHITE HORSE INN

1532 N. WESTERN AVE. (ONE BLOCK NORTH OF HOLLYWOOD), HOLLYWOOD (323) 462-8088. OPEN NIGHTLY, 4 P.M.–2 A.M. FULL BAR. 21 AND OVER. NO COVER. NO FOOD. $.

A big, dark dive that has the feel of a house under construction. No one's going to trek across town to get here, but the jukebox has some good funk, and you're always assured an empty stool. The area's a little shabby (close neighbors include a Pussycat Theater, a psychic and a pawn shop), and there are a dozen more comely bars within a five-minute drive, but if you're driving past, why not? One good quality: you can bring a group and take over the room and no one will bat an eye.

WILDLIFE WAYSTATION

14831 LITTLE TUJUNGA CANYON ROAD, ANGELES NATIONAL FOREST (818) 899-5201. WWW.WAYSTATION.ORG. OPEN NIGHTLY

DURING THE SUMMER; SUN. AFTERNOONS YEAR-ROUND. NO ALCOHOL. ALL AGES. DINNER AND SAFARI, $50; AFTERNOON ADMISSION, $12 FOR ADULTS, $6 FOR CHILDREN. NO FOOD. $$.

Years ago, my ex said he had an unusual and generous friend he wanted me to meet. We drove up the serpentine roads of the Angeles National Forest, and, an hour later, I was introduced to Martine Colette, a small, feisty French gal in a safari outfit who showed us the latest resident of her 1600-acre animal sanctuary—a baby monkey some yahoo had adopted and, apparently feeling the primate too much work, abandoned. For 25 years, Colette's nonprofit Wildlife Waystation has provided safe harbor to unwanted animals. We're not talking a couple of kittens, but over 1,000 wild and exotic animals—lions and tigers and bears, chimps and eagles and alligators—in need of rescuing, relocation, and/or permanent refuge. The Starlight Dinner and Safari Tour (offered every night during the summer) allows visitors to safely come within feet of ferocious beasts and cuddly critters. Bring the kids for a tour Sunday afternoons (year-round).

WORLD STAGE

4344 DENGAN BLVD. (ONE BLOCK EAST OF CRENSHAW), LEIMERT PARK (323) 293-2451. OPEN NIGHTLY, 9 P.M. UNTIL LATE. NO ALCOHOL. ALL AGES. COVER VARIES. NO FOOD. $.

A stark white room that looks like an art gallery without any art, filled with folding chairs on which to park yourself and listen to what can be excellent jazz by solid acts and up-and-comers. Stay late enough, and you might find yourself in the company of some huge-name players who've been known to drop by after an uptown gig to jam until the wee hours. Interesting crowd (men in dashikis, guys in Dockers, little kids); bring someone who's tired of flash and ready to spend a little time with the genuine article.

YAMASHIRO

1999 N. SYCAMORE AVE. (ABOVE FRANKLIN, BETWEEN LA BREA AND HIGHLAND) (323) 466-5125. BAR OPEN SUN.–THURS., 4:30 P.M.–12:30 A.M.; SAT. AND SUN., 4:40 P.M.–1:30 A.M. FULL BAR. ALL AGES. NO COVER. FOOD (JAPANESE). $$$.

If we accept that we are fools for a view, it's easy to appreciate the aviary charms of Yamashiro, a Japanese restaurant and bar with a sweeping panorama of the city. Begin in the traditional Japanese bar, but make sure you wind up on the dining terrace, surrounded by topiary and reflecting pools overlooking the city, by night a riot of incandescent glitter bordered by black sea. While the food (sushi and Japanese) does not match the view, this should not deter you from bringing people you want to impress: dates, visitors, the grumpy and the landlocked.

YE RUSTIC INN

1831 HILLHURST AVE. (ONE BLOCK SOUTH OF FRANKLIN), LOS FELIZ (323) 662-5757. OPEN DAILY, 6 A.M.–2 A.M. FULL BAR. 21 AND OVER. NO COVER. FOOD (BAR MENU). $.

Let me confess right out: Ye Rustic is my local bar, the place I most often go to have a drink, to watch a basketball game, to shoot the shit with the bartenders. The reasons are simple: everyone here is kind, the drinks are reasonably priced, and though it can get crowded with scenesters on the weekends, regulars usually outnumber them. Dark, with big cozy booths, an always-busy dartboard, a few TVs, and better-than-edible bar food. Every neighborhood should be so lucky.

ZABUMBA

10717 VENICE BLVD. (AT OVERLAND), WEST LA (310) 841-6525. WWW.ZABUMBA.COM. OPEN NIGHTLY, 6 P.M.–2 A.M. BEER AND WINE ONLY. ALL AGES. NO COVER SUN.–THURS.; FRI. AND SAT. AFTER 9:30 P.M., $7. FOOD (LATIN ECLECTIC). $$.

You know those cinematic portrayals of Latin nightclubs, with toucan-colored rooms and horn sections so scorching diners let their *frijoles negros* grow cold in order to grab a stranger by the hips and rhumba around the room? Then you know what you're in for at this Brazilian/Latin club and restaurant, with live music/acts most nights, from Brazilian pop and feather dancers to deejays spinning Cuban sounds. Fabulous and fun, especially with a group.

Late-night Eating

LATE-NIGHT EATING

The criterion for being included on the following list is that the establishment be open late. The quality of the food is above reproach at most of the places, exquisite at some, and at others merely passable. All will feed you past midnight, most for under $12.

APPLE PAN

10801 PICO BLVD. (EAST OF WESTWOOD), WEST LA (310) 475-3585. OPEN SUN.–THURS., 11 A.M.–MIDNIGHT; FRI. AND SAT., 11 A.M.–1 A.M. $.

If you discover an hour when the Apple Pan is not packed, please let me know. The enduring popularity of this landmark is due to the fact that they only do a few things—two kinds of burgers, two sandwiches, fries, and a couple of pies—and that they do each of them perfectly. The burgers are sublime and just greasy enough, and the cool slices of banana cream pie are the sort of iconic fare you daydream about during traffic jams. All served in a vintage diner by waitresses who look as though they may have been working there since the place opened in 1947. Though the line almost always spills onto Pico, it's worth the wait.

ASTRO FAMILY RESTAURANT

2300 FLETCHER DR. (AT GLENDALE), SILVERLAKE (323) 663-9241. OPEN DAILY, 24 HOURS. $.

Let's list the reasons to go to Astro: it's open all the time; its design is classic, with lots of family-size booths and a mile-long counter; the food is reliable American; and they serve breakfast anytime. But what hooks me is the hostess, who wears a floor-length gown, tons of costume jewelry, and enough cosmetics to qualify for a spot on the Tammy Faye team, and who leads you to your table in a *Valley of the Dolls* haze. A nice touch to an extended evening.

BENITO'S TACO SHOP

7912 BEVERLY BLVD. (AT FAIRFAX), LOS ANGELES (323) 938-7427. OPEN DAILY, 24 HOURS. $. ALSO, 1544 S. LA CIENEGA (A QUARTER MILE SOUTH OF PICO) (310) 360-7386; 6751 SANTA MONICA BLVD. (ONE BLOCK EAST OF HIGHLAND), HOLLYWOOD (323) 466-9333.

"Home of the rolled taco," served with little sides of marinated carrots and jalapeños and tangy salsa. Decor at these taco stands runs to a few plastic tables on the street, which can make dining a noisy/on-your-feet experience, but the tacos, burritos, *tortas*, and enchiladas are always fresh, the prices are low, and, because the shops are 24-hour and spread around town, there's usually one open near you.

BOB'S BIG BOY

4211 W. RIVERSIDE DR. (AT ALAMEDA), BURBANK (818) 843-9334. WWW.BOBS.NET. OPEN DAILY, 24 HOURS. $.

The most iconic of all Southern California diners, Bob's opened in 1949, with car-hop service in the parking lot, a 75-foot sign advertising the "original DOUBLE DECK HAMBURGER," and a streamlined Moderne diner that, in 1993, was given the designation "State Point of Historic Interest." You can still get great burgers (and all manner of diner fare), and there's still car-hop service Saturday and Sunday nights. On Friday nights, the parking lot resembles a scene from *American Graffiti*, with auto enthusiasts leaning on the hoods of their cherried-out Model-T's and muscle cars, eyeing one another's rides as they slurp down Cokes.

CANTER'S

419 N. FAIRFAX AVE. (BETWEEN MELROSE AND BEVERLY), FAIRFAX DISTRICT (323) 651-2030. OPEN DAILY, 24 HOURS. $$.

Whatever you think of the food (and plenty of delicatessen connoisseurs—also known as former New Yorkers—swear it's not as good as it should be), Canter's is an institution. It never closes; it serves every manner of corned meat and smoked fish and chicken soup with matzoh balls as big as a baby's head; there's a bakery with good rye and challah and *rugullah* and 100 other sweets; and the giant, murkily lit room is always ringing with a dozen languages coming out of 100 mouths, each trying to get the attention of the ornery waitresses, who'll get to you when they're ready. The scene is worth the trip. The food? Eh.

DAMIANO'S/MR. PIZZA

412 N. FAIRFAX AVE. (BETWEEN MELROSE AND BEVERLY), LOS ANGELES (323) 658-7611. OPEN SUN.–THURS., 10 A.M.–6 A.M.; FRI. AND SAT., 10 A.M.–7 A.M. $.

Damiano's caters to night owls (take a look at their hours, above), New Yorkers desperate for pizza by the slice, and anyone who agrees that anything with inch-thick dough or barbecued chicken slather should not be allowed to call itself pizza. Damiano's is the real thing: thin crust with black blisters on the bottom, and enough grease and cheese to make the slice droop. Visually, the room's nothing to write home about: hot (from the pizza ovens) and narrow, with just a few booths, usually containing disheveled rockers working their way through a pie. You can stand at the counter, sit on a bench out front, or have Damiano's deliver, which they'll do until all hours. (They'll even bring you a bottle of wine.)

DAN TANA'S

9071 SANTA MONICA BLVD. (EAST OF DOHENY), WEST HOLLYWOOD (310) 275-9444. OPEN DAILY, 5 P.M.–1 A.M. $$$.

This landmark restaurant may have an Italian name (and I know a few folks who rave about the chicken parmigiana), but Dan Tana's is as straight-ahead as a steak-and-martini joint gets. The bar is loud, lively, and packed tight every night with seasonal Hollywood players, local politicos, and sports stars, and the dining room is the sort of clubby, old-world place you'd expect to find in Jersey. Get a corner table, bring a fat wallet (Tana's is pricey and worth it), and tuck into what I think is the best steak in LA. Damn good spinach, too.

DENNY'S

7373 SUNSET BLVD. (BETWEEN LA BREA AND FAIRFAX), HOLLYWOOD (323) 876-6660. OPEN DAILY, 24 HOURS. $.

Sure, there's a Denny's off every exit ramp in the United States, but there's only one rock 'n' roll Denny's, where would-be rock gods who've been slinging their axes up the Strip go when appetite reregisters, usually between 3 A.M. and 5 A.M. While the food, color scheme, and layout resemble those of every other Denny's, here the aisles are strewn with guitar cases, patrons' epic early-evening hairdos are reconfigured into shrubbery or spaghetti, and there's usually a little jailbait lightly snoozing beside her eggs. A little high life with that Grand Slam?

DU-PAR'S

12036 VENTURA BLVD. (AT LAUREL CANYON), STUDIO CITY (818) 766-4437. WWW.DUPARS.COM. OPEN MON.–FRI., 6 A.M.–1 A.M.; SAT. AND SUN., 6 A.M.–4 A.M. $. ALSO, FARMER'S MARKET, FAIRFAX AND 3RD ST., LOS ANGELES (323) 933-8446; 8571 SANTA MONICA (JUST EAST OF LA CIENEGA), WEST HOLLYWOOD (310) 659-7009; 75 W. THOUSAND OAKS BLVD. (BETWEEN 101 FWY. AND MOORPARK) (805) 373-8785.

I pledge fealty to this 60-year-old coffeehouse and their butter-drenched, lightly eggy, powdered-sugar-dusted French toast or the equally butter-soaked, plate-sized pancakes, and not because an old tin sign over the kitchen reads, "Hot Cakes Make You Happy!," but because DuPar's makes the best breakfast starches bar none. I also like their pies, which come in a zillion varieties, though my advice is to leave the ho-hum sandwiches and Blue Plate dinners (pot roast, meat loaf, ham steak) to others. (Note: The only branch open late-late is in Studio City, where the crowd tends to be an odd mix of Valley insomniacs. Get some sleep and head for breakfast at the nice, safe DuPar's in the Farmer's Market.)

ELECTRIC LOTUS

4656 Franklin Ave. (at Vermont), Los Feliz (323) 953-0040. Open Sun.–Thurs., 11 a.m.–Midnight; Fri. and Sat., 11 a.m.–1 a.m. $$.

This very popular Los Feliz restaurant features "Village Cuisine from India," a wonderful selection of curries, vegetarian and non-veg, eight kinds of naan, large combination meals that can feed a crowd, and affordable lunch specials. The seductive room, however, is what keeps Electric Lotus packed: booths shrouded in exotic cloths, a private banquet room with low tables and cushioned seating, a deejay spinning music on the weekends, a sexy little wine bar, and a large and beautiful mural of Ganesha overlooking it all and wishing us good appetite.

FRED 62

1850 N. Vermont Ave. (one block south of Franklin), Los Feliz (323) 667-0062. Open daily, 24 hours. $$.

This retro-hipster diner has its finger on the pulse that is Los Feliz: lots of eye-candy (an electric-green facade; wait people with a zillion tattoos), gadgetry (a toaster on every table), comfort (big booths in which to recline/fortify/recover from a hangover), convenient hours (24/7), lots of outdoor tables for people watching, and eclectic victuals: a mean dish of French toast, a complicated Thai salad, a soothing bowl of *udon*, and fresh carrot juice.

GREENBLATT'S

8017 SUNSET BLVD. (BETWEEN FAIRFAX AND CRESCENT HEIGHTS), WEST HOLLYWOOD (323) 656-0606. OPEN DAILY, 9 A.M.–2 A.M. $$.

Greenblatt's offers fine delicatessen (and great chicken broth, with a matzoh ball so light I had to leap up and catch it before it floated away), but the room sort of gives me the creeps. Built in 1926, the place hasn't been redecorated in a while, and it feels ... soiled. Well, never mind; others seem to like it, particularly the crowd that comes from their homes in the Hills/apartments around West Hollywood to read the trades and have a nosh.

HOUSE OF PIES

1869 N. VERMONT AVE. (AT FRANKLIN), LOS FELIZ (323) 666-9961. OPEN SUN.–THURS., 6:30 A.M.–1 A.M.; FRI. AND SAT., 7 A.M.–1 A.M. $.

Los Feliz's local coffee shop/diner, with food that I cannot recommend but that everyone else (including the LAPD: there's at least one squad car in the parking lot at all times) seems to think is fine. The breakfasts are easy to take, as are the pies (note: bringing one as a hostess gift will not cause embarrassment) and items that are hard to get wrong: BLT, tuna on toast, grilled cheese. But get me away from the clam chowder, or anything involving the gravy, which tastes like the lining of a tin can. Fairly bustling in the A.M., with local creative types lingering over the newspaper until lunch, House of Pies is slower and sort of lonely during dinner, with lots of very old folks sitting alone in booths. Things pick up again after 10 P.M., when those who've caught a movie across the street/had a few drinks at the Dresden stop in for a late-night snack.

IN-N-OUT

7009 SUNSET BLVD. (TWO BLOCKS EAST OF HIGHLAND), HOLLYWOOD (800) 786-1000. WWW.IN-N-OUT.COM. OPEN SUN.–THURS., 10:30 A.M.–1 A.M.; FRI. AND SAT., UNTIL 1:30 A.M. $.

There have been many nights when we've left before last call in order to get to In-N-Out before *it* closes. The only reliably excellent fast-food burger I know of—available with grilled onions, if you ask for them. Some people find the fries here a little dry, but I not only love their taste, I love watching the employees hand-dry each batch in a cotton towel. Whee! The only drawback to the Hollywood branch are the lines, which are always long. Make sure to pick up the little map, which gives the locations of the many other In-N-Outs across the southland.

JERRY'S FAMOUS DELI

12655 VENTURA BLVD. (BETWEEN LAUREL CANYON AND COLDWATER CANYON), STUDIO CITY (818) 980-4245. OPEN DAILY, 24 HOURS. $$. ALSO, 8701 BEVERLY BLVD. (BETWEEN SAN VINCENTE AND ROBERTSON) (310) 289-1811; 10923 WEYBURN AVE. (AT WESTWOOD), WESTWOOD VILLAGE (310) 208-3354; AND 13181 MINDANAO WAY (AT LINCOLN), MARINA DEL REY (310) 821-6626. CALL FOR HOURS.

I am tempted to put forth the theory that Jerry's has over 400 items on the tiny-print menu because they're trying to confound you into just ordering, counting on the likelihood that, when you're delivered a mediocre meal, you'll blame yourself for not choosing more carefully. It's not you; the food is not that good; it's also expensive. One plus: the Jerry's in Studio City is right next door to a bowling alley.

JOHNNIE'S PASTRAMI

4017 S. SEPULVEDA BLVD. (BETWEEN WASHINGTON BLVD. AND WASHINGTON PLACE), CULVER CITY (310) 397-6654. OPEN SUN. AND MON., 10 A.M.–1 A.M.; TUES.–THURS., 10 A.M.–2:30 A.M.; FRI. AND SAT., 10 A.M.–3:30 A.M. $.

Now here's a late-night spot worth the drive: a beautiful futuristic Googie building, and a lunch counter with all the original fixtures and some of the best hot and greasy pastrami sandwiches in LA, with slippery blackened rims of fat poking out from between soft rye, and a fat and tasty homemade kosher-style pickle on the side. The atmosphere is as mellow as the food is delicious, with everyone always appearing happy to be here, maybe having a little chat with their neighbor or fiddling with the tabletop jukeboxes. A wonderful place.

JONES. *See listing under "Bars and Clubs."*

KATE MANTILINI

9101 WILSHIRE BLVD. (AT DOHENY), BEVERLY HILLS (310) 278-3699. OPEN MON.–THURS., 7:30 A.M.–1 A.M.; FRI., UNTIL 2 A.M.; SAT., 11 A.M.–2 A.M.; SUN., 10 A.M.–MIDNIGHT. $$$.

Straight lines and steel and glass give this eatery a high art/industrial look. While some complain about attitude, others swear the homey fare—open-faced turkey sandwiches with mashed potatoes; Lemon Icebox Pie—hits the spot. I suspect diners are just as enamored of the beautiful, well-heeled people who pack the place at all hours as they are of the food. But I quibble. In this part of town at this time of night, one is lucky to find anything to eat. Keep the order simple, try to ignore the tab, and enjoy.

KRISPY KREME

7249 VAN NUYS BLVD. (A HALF BLOCK NORTH OF SHERMAN WAY), VAN NUYS (818) 908-9113. WWW.KRISPYKREME.COM. OPEN DAILY, 6 A.M.–MIDNIGHT. $. (THERE ARE MANY KRISPY KREME OUTLETS IN THE WORKS. CLICK ON THEIR WEB SITE FOR CURRENT INF.)

I had my first Krispy Kreme glazed doughnut recently, and damn, it was delicious, tasting exactly like the donuts I used to buy at the Woolworth's in Brooklyn in the seventies. If you want the glazed to be hot (and you do), buy them when the "Hot Doughnuts Now!" sign is flashing, usually between 5 and 10, A.M. and P.M. The ambitious can drive to the La Habra location, which has a 24-hour drive-thru, though continual access to these sweet, airy, disappear-in-a-mouthful confections makes me think they ought to change the sign to "Fat Hips Ahead!"

THE LUNCH TO LATENITE KITCHEN

4348 FOUNTAIN AVE. (AT SUNSET), SILVERLAKE (323) 664-FOOD. OPEN MON.–THURS., 11 A.M.–1 A.M.; FRI., 11 A.M.–4 A.M.; SAT., 10 A.M.–4 A.M.; SUN., 10 A.M.–1 A.M. $$.

While the 1990s saw the neighborhoods of Los Feliz and Silverlake transform from fringe communities to the epicenter of all things arty and fab, and while this metamorphosis naturally gave rise to several dozen new restaurants, with a few exceptions most of these new eateries are just passable. Then, in the summer of 2000, on the border of Los Feliz and Silverlake (a location convenient to everyone), came this funky slip of a room, open when the locals want to eat (see name) and serving the sort of homey fare you'd make yourself if you had the time/inclination/skill: big, steamy bowls of chicken and dumplings; tender, sweet-and-spicy ribs; excellent burgers with super-skinny fries. Very casual (feel like reading the paper for an hour over a cup of coffee and a plate of eggs? No problem) and very friendly, the Lunch to Latenite Kitchen gets my vote for best Eastside place to eat after the clubs close.

MEL'S DRIVE-INN

8585 Sunset Blvd. (west of La Cienega), West Hollywood (310) 854-7200. Open daily, 24 hours. $$.

A 1990s diner putting on the 1950s, with jukeboxes full of oldies at every table and stylistic doo-dads that are supposed to dredge up feelings of nostalgia. Well, whatever. If you like fat burgers and thick shakes, you'll find both at Mel's, along with big booths and a lot of diners getting off on the fact that they're spending time on the Sunset Strip. If I sound a little cranky, it's because Mel's replaced a really great and authentic diner, Ben Frank's.

MO BETTER MEATTY MEAT BURGERS

5855 Pico (at Fairfax) (323) 938-6558. Open Sun.–Thurs., 11 a.m.–midnight; Sat. and Sun., 11 a.m.–3 a.m. $.

An urban burger stand serving seven-ounce blackened-on-the-outside, rare-on-the-inside, lashed-with-mayo-and-all-the-fixings, what-a-delicious-mess-this-is burgers. While I'm not crazy about the fat pale fries (though the sprinkling of black pepper's a nice idea), or the onion rings (frozen variety), I do like the covered patio, where two mounted TVs continuously show the news or game shows or basketball. If you go in the afternoon, you'll eat amid school kids doing their homework between bites of burger and peeks at the tube.

NOVA EXPRESS. *See listing under "Bars and Clubs."*

NYC SEAFOOD

715 W. GARVEY AVE. (AT ATLANTIC), MONTEREY PARK (626) 289-9898. OPEN DAILY, 11:30 A.M.–3 A.M. $$.

A Hong Kong–style restaurant in the center of the Monterey Park dining district, celebrated for the freshest seafood: massive prawns are scooped from tanks and steamed moments before they're served, sweet and nearly translucent. All the seafood is fresh as can be, and there are some magnificent vegetarian offerings as well, especially the Eggplant Hot Pot (which we always wind up ordering twice, after the first order is scarfed down by people who'd heretofore sworn the purple nightshade a mortal enemy). Excellent place to bring a group, including someone who reads Chinese: wall banners written in Chinese characters offer dishes not translated on the menu.

ORIGINAL PANTRY CAFÉ

877 S. FIGUEROA ST. (AT 9TH), DOWNTOWN LA (213) 972-9279. OPEN DAILY, 24 HOURS. $$.

I like the idea of this all-American greasy spoon—opened in 1924, currently owned by Mayor Riordan—more than I like the actual experience, which, last time I waited in line an hour to eat, was disastrous: a layer of grime on everything, a waiter who knocked a water glass into my lap, eggs that had to be sent back . . . twice. How hard is it to fry eggs? Ah, well, I've also had good meals here, sitting at the counter, watching line-cooks hustle through the steam to pile plates with pork chops and hash browns. Good or bad, the Pantry holds true to its motto, "Never closed, never without a customer." Many of the customers are tourists eager to get a taste of historic LA/take home a commemorative mug.

ORIGINAL TOMMY'S

2575 BEVERLY BLVD. (AT RAMPART), LOS ANGELES (213) 389-9060. WWW.ORIGINALTOMMYS.COM. OPEN DAILY, 24 HOURS. $. 18 OTHER LOCATIONS IN SOUTHERN CALIFORNIA.

Anyone new to Los Angeles wonders why there are so many hamburger joints incorporating the name Tommy. Eventually they wind up at an Original Tommy's, and realize it's because any would-be burger baron with half a brain wants to trick people into thinking he's the one who invented the Tommy Burger, a two-handed beauty, slippery with chili, two slices of cheese, and enough good grease to soak your cuffs. Tamales, hot dogs, and good fries, sure, but it's the burgers that have kept Tommy's packed, round the clock, for 50 years. Great hangover food. Just eat one of these and head back to bed.

PACIFIC DINING CAR

1310 W. 6TH ST. (BETWEEN ALVARADO AND FIGUEROA), DOWNTOWN LA (213) 483-6000. WWW.PACIFICDININGCAR.COM. OPEN DAILY, 24 HOURS. $$$. ALSO, 2700 WILSHIRE BLVD. (BETWEEN BUNDY AND 26TH ST.), SANTA MONICA (310) 453-4000. OPEN DAILY, 6 A.M.–2 A.M.

A plush, expanded steak house in a railway car, opened in 1921, the PDC is the place to devour beef with the wanton abandon of a turn-of-the-century robber baron. While the prices might make you flinch (two of us recently spent $130—on lunch), the "USDA Prime, Eastern Corn-

Fed Beef" is truly fine, as are the omelettes and other breakfast offerings. Many of the customers look as though they've been eating here since the place opened, and the feel is definitely old-world men's club, an urbane time tunnel that makes one loath to return to the contemporary world of shabby 99¢ burgers. A splurge and a must.

PALMS THAI RESTAURANT

5273 HOLLYWOOD BLVD. (BETWEEN WESTERN AND NORMANDIE, AT HOBART), HOLLYWOOD (323) 462-5073. WWW.PALMSTHAI.COM. OPEN DAILY, 11 A.M.–2 A.M. $$.

A lively Thai restaurant serving excellent noodles and curries and soups, plus an amazing array of "Wild Things," like Frogs with Crispy Mint Leaves and Deer with Spicy Sauce. Even if you stick to Pad Thai, you'll be happy at Palms, as one end of the room sports a big elevated stage, where, depending on the evening, you'll see Kavee Thongpricha, also known as Calvin the Thai Elvis, in a skintight rhinestone jumpsuit, beautifully working his way through the King's oeuvre; a Thai rock band; or balladeers like the guy who sang "American Pie" so faithfully, I thought he was lip-synching.

PHO WESTERN

425 S. WESTERN AVE. (BETWEEN 4TH AND 5TH), KOREATOWN (213) 387-9100. OPEN DAILY, 24 HOURS. $.

Small, clean *pho* (beef broth with noodles) shop with a tiny menu: six types of *pho*, served with the traditional complements of bean sprouts, Thai basil, and sliced chilis; soft-skinned summer rolls; iced Vietnamese coffee. Soothing and simple, except right after the clubs close, when it can become a zoo.

PINK'S

709 N. La Brea Ave. (just north of Melrose), West Hollywood (323) 931-4223. Open Sun.–Thurs., 9:30 a.m.–2 a.m.; Fri. and Sat., 9:30 a.m.–3 a.m. $.

A humble stand serving incredible hot dogs (with or without unctuous umber chili, or with cheese, or crammed with jalepeños, or . . .). Grab a few dogs, a plate of baked fries, and a Dr. Brown's, and gorge on the little outdoor patio, or right on the sidewalk, with the throngs who've made Pink's an institution.

PIPERS

222 N. Western (just south of Beverly), Koreatown (323) 465-7701. Open daily, 24 hours. $.

Cool and courtly coffeehouse/restaurant with a Camelot/Mt. Olympus decor: a suit of armor in the entryway, swords and shields on the walls, lion-topped columns separating the large, exceptionally clean dining room. Great big booths, reliably good breakfasts and burgers, and daily dinner specials from beef Bourguignonne to franks and beans. A tranquil place to hide out: I've never seen the place crowded, the wait staff doesn't rush you, and there's classical music playing at all times.

ROSCOE'S HOUSE OF CHICKEN AND WAFFLES

1514 N. Gower St. (just north of Sunset), Hollywood (323) 466-7453. www.chickenandwaffles.com. Open Mon.–Thurs., 8:30 a.m.–Midnight; Fri. and Sat., 8:30 a.m.–4 a.m.; Sun., noon–midnight. $$. Other locations: 5006 W. Pico Blvd. (west of La Brea), Mid-City (323) 934-4405; 830 N. Lake Ave. (between Orange Grove and Mountain), Pasadena (626) 752-6211; 106 W. Manchester Ave. (at Main), South Central LA (323) 752-6211.

The combo here is amazing: incredible fried chicken that comes with a malty/cinnamony waffle topped with a scoop of butter. The only problem is, you have to really be hungry; when I ask people if they want to eat at Roscoe's, they often begin to look afraid. Cowards. I make it here as often as possible, and if I can stay away from the fried chicken (which is not often), I go for a plate of chicken smothered with gravy and onions, and two waffles. Then I go for a run.

SANAMLUANG

5176 Hollywood Blvd. (between Western and Normandie), Hollywood (323) 660-8006. Open daily, 10 a.m.–5 a.m. $.

I noticed that Sanamluang recently erected a canopy that reads "The Best Noodles in Town." Many agree, making this informal Thai restaurant one of the most popular hangouts in LA, especially after 2 A.M., when every partyer within ten miles thinks it might be a good idea to eat a little something before bed. Why not General's Noodles (with barbecued pork, roast duck, and shrimp), or an Indian curry with coconut milk, or one of their wonderful soups, brimming with dumplings and fish balls?

SUEHIRO

337 E. 1st St. (east of San Pedro), Little Tokyo (213) 626-9132. Open Sun.–Thurs., 11 a.m.–1 a.m.; Fri. and Sat., 11 a.m.–3 a.m. $.

A utilitarian noodle house (with a lunch counter) that serves all kinds of noodles—*udon, ramen, somen, soba*—plus other Japanese and "Chinese-style" dishes. In the heart of Little Tokyo, it's a stone's throw from both the Geffen Temporary/Contemporary and Japanese American museums, and one of the cleaner Downtown spots for chow after 2 A.M.

SWINGERS

Beverly Laurel Motor Hotel, 8020 Beverly Blvd. (one block east of Crescent Heights), Los Angeles (323) 653-5858. Open daily, 6:30 a.m.–4 a.m. $$.

I don't believe there's a hip barometer mounted on the door of this faux-retro diner, but there might as well be. The young, expensively scruffy patrons have their looks down pat: just-so-mussed gym attire, this season's cool dog tied to an outdoor table, laptops scrolling through spec scripts. The food is actually good—diner fare and many health-conscious offerings—but it's the scene-and-be-seen factor that keeps the place packed.

TOI

7505½ Sunset Blvd. (between Fairfax and La Brea), West Hollywood (323) 874-8062. Open daily, 11 a.m.–4 a.m. $$.

For years, Toi has been a destination after the bars close and you want the party to continue. Yes, the Thai menu is varied, and the food is good, but it's the room that appeals to the young and hungry crowd: animal prints and posters and rock 'n' roll memorabilia and loud music.

TV CAFÉ

1777 E. Olympic Blvd. (at Alameda), Downtown LA (213) 624-1155. Open daily, 24 hours. $.

A trucker diner on a miniature scale, with cheap taco plates and burgers, lots of video and arcade games, and plastic booths with seats as hard as the back of an LAPD squad car. Recommended for the truly famished.

Bars, Clubs, and Dining by Location

BARS AND CLUBS

ANAHEIM
Memories

ATWATER/GLENDALE
The Bigfoot Lodge
Cinnabar
Club Tee Yee
Damon's Steakhouse
Jax Bar and Grill
The Roost

BEVERLY HILLS
C Bar
Coconut Club
Four Seasons Windows
    Lounge
Nic's
Polo Lounge
Trader Vic's
   Dining:
   Dan Tana's
   Kate Mantilini

BURBANK
The Blue Room
Viva Cantina
   Dining:
   Bob's Big Boy

CHATSWORTH
Cowboy Palace
    Saloon

CHINATOWN/LITTLE TOKYO
Grand Star
Hop Louie
   Dining:
   Suehiro

CULVER CITY
The Culver Saloon
Jazz Bakery
   Dining:
   Johnnie's Pastrami

DOWNTOWN LA
Al's Bar
Grand Avenue
Hank's
King Edward Saloon
The Lab
Regal Biltmore, Gallery
    Bar
Sam's Hofbrau
The Smell
Traxx
   Dining:
   Original Pantry Café
   Pacific Dining Car
   TV Café

EAGLE ROCK/HIGHLAND PARK
All Star Lanes
Mr. T's Bowl

BARS, CLUBS, AND DINING BY LOCATION

ECHO PARK

Little Joy

Dining:
Original Tommy's

FAIRFAX DISTRICT

Canter's Kibitz Room
Farmer's Market Bars—
    EB's and 326
Ghengis Cohen
Largo
Max's Bar and Lounge
Molly Malone's
Nova Express
Tom Bergin's

Dining:
Benito's Taco Shop
Canter's
Damiano's/Mr. Pizza
Du-Par's

HOLLYWOOD

The Baked Potato
    Hollywood
Beauty Bar
Blacklite Cocktail
    Room
Boardner's
Burgundy Room
Catalina Bar and Grill
The Cat 'n' Fiddle
Cherry. *(See under "The*
    Playroom.")
Cinegrill Cabaret and
    Lounge
Crazy Girls
The Crush Bar
Daddy's
Deep
Les Deux Café
Dragonfly
El Floridita
Frolic Room
Garden of Eden
The Gig Hollywood
Goldfingers
Hollywood Billiards
Hollywood Star Lanes
Jumbo's Clown Room
Kane
The Knitting Factory
    Hollywood
Las Palmas Supper Club
Lava Lounge
Louis XIV
Martini Lounge
Miceli's
Ming's Dynasty
Musso & Frank Grill
Opium Den
Pinot Hollywood
The Playroom
La Poubelle
Power House
The Room
The Ruby

The Spot Light Club
Sunset Room
360°
Three of Clubs
Tiki Theater
Tommy Tang's
Vynyl
White Horse Inn
Yamashiro
Dining:
Benito's Taco Shop
Denny's
In-N-Out Burger
Palms Thai Restaurant
Roscoe's House of Chicken and Waffles
Sanamluang

KOREATOWN
Frank N Hank's
Dining:
Pho Western
Piper's

LEIMERT PARK
Babe's & Ricky's Inn
World Stage

LOS ANGELES
El Carmen
Cava
Dominick's
Fais Do-Do
Gabah
The Mint
Dining:
Benito's Taco Shop
Jerry's Famous Deli
Swingers

LOS FELIZ
Bar Vermont
Cheetahs
The Derby
The Drawing Room
Dresden Room
Good Luck
Jazz Spot
Vida
Ye Rustic Inn
Dining:
Fred 62
House of Pies
The Lunch to Latenite Kitchen

MID-CITY
Jewel's Catch One
Lowenbrau Keller Restaurant
Voodoo
Dining:
Mo Better Meatty Meat Burgers

Roscoe's House of Chicken and Waffles

MID-WILSHIRE
The Atlas Supper Club
Brass Monkey
La Fonda de Los Camperos
H.M.S. Bounty

MIRACLE MILE
The Conga Room
El Rey Theater

MONTEREY PARK
Dining:
NYC Seafood

NORTH HOLLYWOOD/SHERMAN OAKS/VAN NUYS/ANGELES NATIONAL FOREST
The Blue Saloon
Casa Vega
Wildlife Waystation
Dining:
Krispy Kreme

SANTA MONICA/VENICE
Bob Burns
Casa del Mar
Chez Jay
Circle Bar
Father's Office
Firehouse
Hal's
Harvelle's
The Red Garter
The Room SM
Shutters, Lobby Bar
Temple Bar
Voda
Dining:
Pacific Dining Car

SILVERLAKE
Akbar
El Chavo
El Cid
The Garage
Red Lion Tavern
Rudolpho's
Silverlake Lounge/Fold
Smog Cutter
Spaceland
Tiki-Ti
Dining:
Astro Family Restaurant
The Lunch to Latenite Kitchen

STUDIO CITY/UNIVERSAL CITY/NORTH HOLLYWOOD
The Baked Potato
B.B. King's Blues Club

Oil Can Harry's
The Queen Mary Night Club
Residuals
Sportsmen's Lodge
    Muddy Moose Bar and Grill
    Dining:
    Du-Par's
    Jerry's Famous Deli

WESTCHESTER
Encounter

WEST HOLLYWOOD
Barfly
Bar Marmont
Barney's Beanery
Club 7969/Peanuts
The Coach & Horses
Coconut Teazer
Dublin's Pub
El Compadre
El Coyote
Fenix Bar
Formosa Café
House of Blues
Jones
J. Sloan's
Key Club
Le Colonial
Lola's
Mamagaya
Normandie Room
North
The Palms
Rage
Roxy
Sky Bar
Stonewall Gourmet Coffee
Tempest
Troubadour
The Viper Room
Whiskey Bar
Whisky a GoGo
Dining:
Du-Par's
Greenblatt's
Mel's Drive-In
Pink's
Toi

WEST LA/CULVER CITY
The Gig West LA
The Joint
The Joker
Liquid Kitty
McCabe's
Zabumba
Dining:
Apple Pan
Jerry's Famous Deli

Bars and Clubs, by Type of Music

While the following will give you an idea of what type of music a club often features, many venues mix it up: rock one night, punk the next, hip-hop the following. If you want to be sure, phone ahead, or look in the *LA Weekly* to see what the lineup is.

BIG BAND/SWING
The Atlas Supper Club
Coconut Club
The Derby
Memories

BLUES
Babe's & Ricky's Inn
The Baked Potato
The Baked Potato Hollywood
B.B. King's Blues Club
The Culver Saloon
Harvelle's
House of Blues
Jax Bar and Grill
The Mint

COUNTRY AND WESTERN
Cowboy Palace and Saloon
The Culver Saloon
Oil Can Harry's
Viva Cantina

ECLECTIC
Boardner's
Canter's Kibitz Room
Dragonfly
Fais Do Do
Gabah
The Garage
The Gig Hollywood
The Gig West LA
Goldfingers
House of Blues
The Joint
Key Club
The Knitting Factory Hollywood
Lava Lounge
Le Colonial
Louis XIV
Martini Lounge
Opium Den
Roxy
Spaceland
Troubadour
The Viper Room

FOLK
Ghengis Cohen
The Knitting Factory Hollywood
McCabe's Guitar Shop
Molly Malone's

Hip-Hop/Funk

Dragonfly
Gabah
The Joint
The Knitting Factory Hollywood
Louis XIV
Mamagaya
The Room
Temple Bar
Vynyl

Jazz

The Atlas Supper Club
The Baked Potato
The Baked Potato Hollywood
Catalina Bar and Grill
Cinegrill Cabaret and Lounge
Ghengis Cohen
Jax Bar and Grill
Jazz Bakery
Jazz Spot
Lava Lounge
The Mint
World Stage

Latin/Mariachi

Cava
The Conga Room
El Cid
El Compadre
El Floridita
Grand Avenue
La Fonda de Los Camperos
Mamagaya
Zabumba

Piano Bars

Bob Burns
Cinegrill Cabaret and Lounge
Jax
Les Deux Café
Miceli's

Punk/Garage

Al's Bar
Dragonfly
Gabah
The Garage
The Knitting Factory Hollywood
The Lab
Mr. T's Bowl
Opium Den
Silverlake Lounge/Fold
The Smell
Spaceland

Rock

The Blue Saloon
Coconut Teazer

Dragonfly
Gabah
The Garage
The Gig Hollywood
The Gig West LA
Goldfingers
The Joint
Key Club
The Knitting Factory
   Hollywood
Martini Lounge
Opium Den
Roxy
Spaceland
Troubadour

The Viper Room
Vynyl
Whisky a GoGo

ROCKABILLY

All Star Lanes
Al's Bar
The Culver
   Saloon
The Garage
The Mint
Mr. T's Bowl
Rudolpho's
The Viper Room

Bars and Clubs by Type of Scene and Other Categories

All Ages

All Star Lanes
The Baked Potato
The Baked Potato Hollywood
Bar Marmont
Barney's Beanery
Bob Burns
Casa Vega
Catalina Bar and Grill
Chez Jay
Cinnabar
Damon's Steak House
Dominick's
El Compadre
El Coyote
Encounter
Fais Do-Do
Farmer's Market Bars— EB's and 326
Firehouse
Four Seasons Windows Lounge
Ghengis Cohen
Hal's
Hollywood Billiards
Hollywood Star Lanes
Jax Bar and Grill
Jazz Bakery
Jazz Spot
The Knitting Factory Hollywood
La Poubelle
Largo
Lowenbrau Keller Restaurant
McCabe's Guitar Shop
Memories
Miceli's
The Mint
Musso and Frank's
Nova Express
Roxy
Tommy Tang's
Trader Vic's
Troubadour
Vida
Viva Cantina
Whisky a GoGo
Wildlife Waystation
World Stage
Yamashiro
Zabumba

Cabaret/Performance

The Atlas Supper Club
Cinegrill Cabaret and Lounge
The Knitting Factory
The Lab
Largo
Le Colonial
LunaPark

The Queen Mary Night
    Club
The Smell

CAFÉ SOCIETY
La Poubelle
Largo
Le Colonial
Les Deux Café
Lola's

DANCING
The Atlas Supper Club
Boardner's
Cherry. *(See listing under "The Playroom.")*
Club 7969/Peanuts
Coconut Club
Cowboy Palace Saloon
The Crush Bar
The Culver Saloon
Deep
The Derby
Dragonfly
El Floridita
El Rey Theater
Fais Do-Do
Gabah
Grand Avenue
Harvelle's
Jewel's Catch One
Key Club
Louis XIV
Make-Up. *(See listing under "El Rey Theater.")*
Martini Lounge
Memories
Oil Can Harry's
Opium Den
The Playroom
Rage
The Ruby
Rudolpho's
Sunset Room
360°
Voodoo
Vynyl
Zabumba

DIVE BARS
Al's Bar
Club Tee Yee
The Coach and Horses
The Drawing Room
Frolic Room
Hop Louie
The Joker
King Edward Saloon
Little Joy
Ming's Dynasty
Mr. T's Bowl
Power House
The Red Garter
Silverlake Lounge/Fold

Smog Cutter
The Spot Light Club
White Horse Inn

Drag/Drag Shows
Dragstrip 66. *(See listing under "Rudolpho's.")*
Make-Up. *(See listing under "El Rey Theater.")*
The Queen Mary Night Club
Tommy Tang's (Tues.)

18 and Over
... meaning, some nights people under 21 are admitted.
C Bar
Club 7969/Peanuts
Coconut Teaszer
The Playroom
Rage
The Ruby
Tempest

Gay/Lesbian
... meaning, more than the usual 10%–20%.
Akbar
Blacklite Cocktail Room
Jewel's Catch One
Ming's Dynasty
Normandie Room
Oil Can Harry's
The Palms
The Queen Mary Night Club
Rage
Rudolpho's
Spot Light
Stonewall Gourmet Coffee
360°

Golden Calf
Barfly
Bar Marmont
Garden of Eden
Sky Bar

Good Looks
... meaning, possessing unusual and/or unique aesthetic oomph.
Bar Vermont
The Bigfoot Lodge
C Bar
Cinnabar
Deep
The Derby
Dominick's
Encounter
Jazz Spot
La Fonda de Los Camperos
Lava Lounge
Le Colonial

Les Deux Café
Lowenbrau Keller
Mamagaya
Musso & Frank Grill
North
Nova Express
Regal Biltmore, Gallery Bar
Tiki-Ti
Yamashiro

Goth
... meaning, venue hosts the occasional goth club.
Boardner's
The Gig Hollywood
The Ruby
Tempest

Historic
Cinegrill Cabaret and Lounge
El Coyote
Formosa Café
Hank's
Musso & Frank Grill
Polo Lounge
Regal Biltmore, Gallery Bar
Whisky a GoGo

Karaoke
Brass Monkey
Farmer's Market Bars—
   EB's and 326

Grand Star
Jewel's Catch One
The Queen Mary Night Club
Residuals
Smog Cutter

LA Experience
Barfly
Bar Marmont
Fenix Bar
Lola's
Musso & Frank Grill
Polo Lounge
Sunset Room
Yamashiro

Lap of Luxury
Casa del Mar
Les Deux Café
Four Seasons Windows Lounge
Polo Lounge
Regal Biltmore, Gallery Bar
Sunset Room

Lounges
Beauty Bar
The Bigfoot Lodge
Burgundy Room
Circle Bar

Daddy's
Dresden Room
El Carmen
Encounter
Formosa Café
Goldfingers
Good Luck
Grand Star
Jones
Kane
Lava Lounge
Liquid Kitty
Max's Bar and Lounge
North
The Room S.M.
Three of Clubs

Model Spotting
Barfly
Bar Marmont
Deep
Dominick's
Fenix Bar
Las Palmas Supper Club
Le Colonial
Sky Bar
Sunset Room
360°
The Viper Room

Neighborhood Spots
Akbar
Bar Vermont
The Blue Room
The Blue Saloon
Brass Monkey
Casa Vega
Cheetahs
Cinnabar
Circle Bar
The Coach and Horses
The Culver Saloon
The Drawing Room
Dresden Room
El Chavo
El Compadre
Father's Office
Firehouse
Frank N Hank's
Hal's
J. Sloan's
Miceli's
Normandie Room
The Red Garter
Red Lion Tavern
Residuals
The Roost
Ye Rustic Inn

No Booze
McCabe's Guitar Shop
The Smell
Stonewall Gourmet Coffee
Tiki Theater
Wildlife Waystation
World Stage

OLD MAN BARS

...meaning, there are usually a few old guys at the bar, a propitious sign.

The Blue Room
Boardner's
Chez Jay
Club Tee Yee
The Coach and Horses
The Drawing Room
Frank N Hank's
Grand Star
Hank's
The H.M.S. Bounty
Hop Louie
King Edward Saloon
Little Joy
Ming's Dynasty
The Roost
Ye Rustic Inn

PICKUP SCENES

...no guarantee.

Barfly
Beauty Bar
The Bigfoot Lodge
Daddy's
Goldfingers
Good Luck
Jones
Kane
La Poubelle
Lava Lounge
Liquid Kitty
Lola's
Opium Den
The Room
The Room S.M.
Sunset Room
The Viper Room

PUBS

The Cat N' Fiddle
Dublin's Pub
Father's Office
J. Sloan's
Molly Malone's
Red Lion Tavern
Tom Bergin's

SCARY

Blacklite Cocktail Room
The Joker
The Spot Light Club
Tiki Theater

SMOKING PERMITTED

*The only bars in California that are legally permitted to allow smoking indoors are those that are owner-operated, and the only one that I know of is the **Tiki-Ti**. This doesn't mean you can't smoke in bars, only that it's against the law—a* *law that many owners flout, as they are of the mind that their customers are their business. You'll know which bars these are as soon as you walk in.*

Sports/Sports Bar/Animals

All Star Lanes
The Blue Saloon
Hollywood Billiards
Hollywood Star Lanes
J. Sloan's
Stonewall Gourmet Coffee (bingo)
Viva Cantina/Sunset Ranch Moonlight Rides
Wildlife Waystation

Strip/Adult Entertainment

Cheetahs
Club 7969/Peanuts
Crazy Girls
Jumbo's Clown Room
Sam's Hofbrau
Tiki Theater

Supper Club

The Atlas Bar and Grill
Catalina Bar and Grill
Cava
Cinegrill Cabaret and Lounge
Jax Bar and Grill
Largo
Las Palmas Supper Club
Memories
The Mint

Tiki

Damon's Steakhouse
Lava Lounge
Tiki-Ti
Trader Vic's

24 Hours

Astro Family Restaurant
Benito's Taco Shop
Bob's Big Boy
Canter's
Denny's
Fred 62
Hollywood Star Lanes
Jerry's Famous Deli
Krispy Kreme (some locations)
Mel's Drive-Inn
Original Pantry
Original Tommy's
Pho Western
Piper's
TV Café

VIEW
Casa del Mar
Shutters, Lobby Bar
Sky Bar
360°
Yamashiro

WACKY/FABULOUS
Brass Monkey
El Cid

Encounter
Lowenbrau Keller Restaurant
Nova Express
The Queen Mary Show Lounge
Wildlife Waystation

Notes

Notes

Notes

Notes